A Food Affair

By
JennyLee Ann Baxter

Copyright © 2022 by – JennyLee Ann Baxter – All Rights Reserved.

It is not legal to reproduce, duplicate, or transmit any part of this document in either electronic means or printed format. Recording of this publication is strictly prohibited.

To Lindsey,
My culinary soul sister!
Bon Appétit,
JennyLee Ann Baxter
December 28, 2022

HOW CAN YOU MAKE ME SO HAPPY?
I DO NOT KNOW.

I JUST KNOW THAT WHEN I AM WITH YOU
I FEEL A BEAUTIFUL GLOW.

AS I TAKE MY MORNING WALKS,
DRINKING IN THE BEAUTIFUL SIGHTS,
I SEE YOUR FACE, AND IT JUST FEELS RIGHT.

AS THE BREEZE WHISPERS THROUGH THE TREES,
I HEAR YOUR VOICE CALLING TO ME,
AMONG THE SWAYING LEAVES.

AS I CROSS THE TRICKLING FALLS,
AND GAZE INTO ITS POOLS,
YOUR SMILE STARES BACK AT ME
AND WARMS MY HEART LIKE A JEWEL.

AS I BEGIN THIS JOURNEY,
THAT I KNOW WILL CHANGE MY LIFE,
I DO SO WITH PATIENCE
AS SO LITTLE STRIFE.

SO I JUST WANT YOU TO KNOW,

AS WE TRAVEL DOWN THIS ROAD,

I WELCOME IT PROUDLY,

AND ANTICIPATE THE MOMENT,

WHEN I AM NO LONGER AFRAID

TO BE ONE WITH YOU,

AS WE LIE UNDER THE STARS,

AMONGST CANDLELIGHT,

AND SMELL THE SCENT OF ROSES,

ON A WARM SUMMER'S NIGHT.

Dedication

This book is dedicated to my father, George Baxter, who always said, "JennyLee, never let any opportunity pass you by!" To my grandmother, Jennie Dahir- Lyons, and my aunt, Betty Johnson, all fine Lebanese cooks, who encouraged me in the kitchen. To my cousin, Linda Malmquist, who inspired me through her own culinary expertise and who shared many of her mouth-watering recipes with me. To Kerry Heckman Bokides, my best friend, whose encouragement and guidance have aided me through the thick and thin parts of my life. To my children, Jaime and Gina Burnsworth, and my precious granddaughter, Victoria, who always appreciate my culinary skills and who love and support me. And to my one true love, Joaquin Santos, whose presence aided my imagination, who created a fire of passion within my soul and his strong love gave me pleasures of the flesh that encouraged my creativity both in the kitchen and the bedroom!

Acknowledgment

First, I would like to thank Paulette Stelte for her tenacious effort in trying to get my book published twenty years ago! Her comments, ideas, and strategies were endless before the time. And then Fifty Shades was released. Next, a thank you to all my YAYA sisters; JoEllen Gano, Agnes Binger, MerryLee DeMaria, Heather Brophy, Lori Deacon, Linda Strangeo- Foster, Pati Barton, Joan Grennell, & Mary Devaney, who helped me get through some tough times, which enabled me to rise again emotionally, so I could write this book. Then, another thanks to Kris Jack, who kept my technology working, so I could communicate with my publisher. Last and not least, a huge thank you to the Amazon publishing team, led by Mathew and Bella, for doing such an outstanding job of publishing A Food Affair!

Author's Bio

JennyLee Ann Baxter
Jenny's Kitchen

- Food Editor *Union Democrat* July 2007
- Featured in *Vine Times* publication February 2007
- Food Columnist *Calaveras Enterprise* February 2007-2022
- Culinary columnist for www.thepinetree.net in addition to "Kids in Jenny's Kitchen" film cooking segments
- Featured in the *Calaveras Enterprise* June 27, 2006
- Featured in the *Stockton Record March 18, 2006*
- Romantic rubs for "*Your Food Affair*" marketed July 2006 "*Hot-N-Horny Bodacious Beef,*" "*Teasing and Pleasing Pork,*" "Passionate *Poultry*," and "*Sensuous Seafood.*"
- Jenny has designed a kitchen tool that will make your life simper. This project is undergoing a feasibility study.
- Author of "*A Food Affair,*" her second cookbook, which Amazon will publish
- Author of "*Jenny Loves Olive Oil*" cookbook published January 2005
- Recipient Calaveras County Best Video Award for "*Jenny's Kitchen*" TV cooking show January 16, 2003
- Guest chef on "*Good Day Sacramento*" UPN channel 31 May 2002
- Cooking Instructor
- Catering and events coordinator

- Author of a quarterly cooking newsletter, "*News from Jenny's Kitchen.*"
- Food consultant and food designer since 1987
- Food demonstration presenter at Calaveras County Fair Cooking Division 1999-2006
- Star of her TV cooking show, "*Jenny's Kitchen,*" shown in Sacramento, Calaveras, Tuolumne, and Amador Counties.
- Book signing at Barnes and Noble Book Store Sacramento March 1999
- Featured in "*For Love of Wine*" newsletter April 2000
- Featured in *Sunset* annual cookbook December 1998
- Featured in *Sunset Magazine* December 1998 issue for Christmas dinner
- Featured in the *Calaveras Enterprise,* the *Union Democrat,* the *Ledger Dispatch,* the *Calaveras Californian,* the *Sierra Sentinel,* the *Stockton Record,* and the *Modesto Bee*
- Food editor *Copperopolis Telegram* 1995
- Proprietress of "*A Catered Affair*" since 1987, now known as "*Jenny's Kitchen.*"
- Food Columnist for The Sierra Lodestar since its inception
- Food Editor of "The Dining Car"
- Food Columnist Highway 4 News

Jenny Baxter
www.jennyskitchen.com
jenny@jennyskitchen.com

Table of Contents

Dedication 4
Acknowledgment 5
Author's Bio 6
Introduction 1
CHAPTER ONE 2
    CLANDESTINE ENCOUNTERS— *Appetizers*
CHAPTER TWO 29
    WARM-HEARTED AFFAIR— *Soup*
CHAPTER THREE 49
    FLIRTY FIRSTS— *Salad*
CHAPTER FOUR 68
    RISING DESIRES— *Breads*
CHAPTER FIVE 85
    SOMETHING ON THE SIDE— *Side Dishes*
CHAPTER SIX 100
    STEAMY ENCOUNTERS— *Vegetables*
CHAPTER SEVEN 120
    HOT AND HEAVIES— *Entrees*
CHAPTER EIGHT 153
    THE MORNING AFTER— *Breakfast*
CHAPTER NINE 170
    WET AND WILD— *Beverages*
CHAPTER TEN 182
    FIRE OF DESIRE— *Condiments*
CHAPTER ELEVEN 194

MOONLIGHT MORSELS FOR TWO— *Midnight Snacks*

CHAPTER TWELVE.. **206**

BITTERSWEET GOOD-BYES— *Dessert*

CHAPTER THIRTEEN **224**

LET FOOD BE YOUR FOREPLAY, AND FOREPLAY BE YOUR FOOD

Introduction

Food and love go hand in hand. They evoke the same passionate feelings. When you indulge, you feel satisfied, warm, happy, comforted, peaceful, relaxed, soothed, grateful, safe, loved, complete, and at times, erotic.

For several years my vision was to write a fabulous cookbook. As my food expertise expanded, which encompassed owning my own catering company, which included food consulting and design; my feature in a national magazine, namely Sunset Magazine and the Sunset Annual Cookbook, my first book signing at Barnes and Noble Books, my own television cooking show, author of a quarterly cooking newsletter, guest chef appearances on "Good Day Sacramento" and a cooking instructor, I was certain that my cookbook was on the horizon.

But, as life would have it, my father, George Baxter, who was my first love, expired in 1996. In January of 1998, my husband of many years and I divorced. In April of that same year, I was diagnosed with Thyroid cancer.

My heart was broken, but my spirit survived!

My life took on new meaning, and this cookbook is the result of the revival of my passion.

The recipes in this cookbook were developed by love for love. Recreate them from your heart, and they will bring you love.

-JennyLee Ann Baxter

CHAPTER ONE
CLANDESTINE ENCOUNTERS
Appetizers

There in the distance, I saw a handsome stranger fly-fishing across the secluded alpine lake, the serene breeze gently sweeping over his masculine silhouette. My intuition was to invite him to sample exciting appetizers set by the shore as he walked toward me, carrying his catch of the day. Forbidden fantasies and food inspire my culinary imagination.

Kiss of Seafood Sausage with Mango Dipping Sauce

Kissing my darling as the old tattered fishing boat set out to sea was the first fantasy I envisioned as I watched his muscular arms tighten and release the fishing line. As I closed my eyes, I could imagine the salty mist gently spraying us. Just as fishing nets were placed deep into the ocean to retrieve treasures from the sea, I could only romanticize the way he would plunge his warm moist tongue deep into my mouth. The treasure he would offer me would far surpass any cache found in the sea.

Sausage
- ½ lb. bay scallops
- 2 tablespoons capers
- 8 oz. salmon fillet
- 4 tablespoons lemon zest
- 4 oz. lobster chopped
- 1 tablespoon chopped fresh dill
- 1 cup white wine & water
- 1/3 cup diced sun-dried tomatoes
- ½ cup Panko breadcrumbs

- 1 beaten egg with 2 tablespoons Pernod
- ¼ lb. crabmeat
- bunch chives snipped
- ½ lb. shrimp meat
- ½ cube butter

Poach the salmon, scallops, and lobster in the wine and water for 15-20 minutes or until the fish easily flakes with the tines of a fork. Place in a bowl and set aside to cool. When cooled, finely mince the mixture and add the crab and shrimp meat. Add the remaining ingredients, except the butter, and thoroughly combine. Melt the butter in a frying pan. When the butter begins to bubble, add the sausage and fry on both sides until the sausage is heated thoroughly. Remove and place on a serving platter placing the dipping sauce in the shell of the mango.

To form the sausages, place a ¼ cup of the mixture in the palm of your hand. Roll this into a ball. If the mixture is a little sticky, add more breadcrumbs, a tablespoon at a time, until the mixture becomes workable. Then flatten the sausage with both hands.
Makes 10 appetizers

Mango Dipping Sauce
- 2 mangos peeled & chopped (reserve the shells)
- 2 tablespoons superfine sugar
- ¼ cup orange juice
- 1 tablespoon orange vinegar
- Pinch red pepper flakes grated ginger
- 1 tablespoon grated coconut

Place the mangos, sugar, vinegar, and orange juice in the bowl of a processor and process until smooth. Remove from the bowl and place the mixture into a serving bowl. Fold in the ginger and red pepper flakes. Sprinkle the coconut on the top. *Makes one cup*

Heart of My Heart Cream Cheese & Wasabi Caviar atop Heart-shaped Cucumbers and Crackers

One afternoon, while visiting the Pacific Coast, I spotted my dream darling digging for clams in the wet sand. I had visions of him placing the warm sand over my naked body and seductively rubbing me down. Then after a thorough leisure showering, we would lounge in our white terry cloth robes as we watched the sailboats glide past the picture window. As we talked about the pleasure of feeling the sun warm our bare backs, we would smell the heady scent that only the ocean can impart. Before we knew it, we would both be aroused. As he held me ever so gently, he whispered in my ear how he wanted to take in my scent as he breathed in the combination of me and the sea. All our senses would then experience illicit delights.

Spread:
- 18 oz package cream cheese softened
- 1 teaspoon white Worcestershire sauce
- 1 tablespoon cream
- ¼ teaspoon ground white pepper
- 1 pinch salt

Combine the above ingredients in a glass bowl. Refrigerate the spread for 1 hour.

- 1 bunch baby dill
- 10 heart-shaped crackers
- 1 English cucumber with the ends removed

- 1 jar Wasabi caviar

Cut ten half- inch thick rounds from an English cucumber. Reserve the remaining cucumber for another use. Using a mini heart-shaped cookie cutter, cut a heart from each round. Place the cucumber hearts on a platter with the heart-shaped crackers. Remove the spread from the refrigerator. Place a half-teaspoon of the spread in the center of each heart-shaped cucumber and cracker. Place a quarter teaspoon of Wasabi caviar on top of the spread. Garnish each cutout with a tiny sprig of baby dill. *Makes 20 appetizers*

Heart-Shaped Crackers:
- 1 package yeast
- 1 ½ cups flour
- ½ teaspoon barley malt
- ¼ teaspoon baking powder
- 1/3 cup warm water
- 2 tablespoons salted butter melted
- 1 tablespoon Romano cheese
- 1 tablespoon butter

In a pitcher, dissolve the yeast and barley malt in the water. Combine the remaining ingredients, except for the butter, in a separate bowl. Place the ingredients in the bowl of a processor. Add the yeast mixture through the feed tube and continue to process until the dough forms a ball around the bowl. Remove the dough from the bowl and wrap it in plastic wrap. Place in the refrigerator for 1 hour. Divide the dough in half and roll each half with a rolling pin into a rectangle about 9 x 12 inches. Fold the dough into thirds and roll again into a 9 x 12 rectangle. Using a 3" heart-shaped cookie cutter, cut the dough into heart shapes. Prick each heart with the tines of a fork. Butter a cookie sheet with a tablespoon of butter. Preheat the oven to 400 degrees. Arrange the crackers on the cookie sheet and bake in the oven for six to eight minutes. Remove from the oven and brush the tops with two tablespoons of melted butter. Crackers may be seasoned with salt, paprika, or more grated cheese at this point. Store the crackers in an airtight container when cool. *Yields 12 crackers*

Halibut Pate to Please

As I sat at the lake's shore, watching the azure water drift in and out, my thoughts slipped into a reverie of wanting to meet this stranger. I allowed my mind to wander toward yet another erotic fantasy. I was slowly becoming obsessed with my desires. As the fiery sun set beyond the green rolling hills casting its multitude of colorful hues upon the ripples in the water, I thought about how we would watch the fish jump as the ducks gleaned across the lake, beckoning us to frolic in the water. Before I knew it, we were swimming to the tiny, west shore cove. Lying upon the warm flat rocks, our naked bodies still dripping, he slides his tongue up and down my flesh from the back of my neck to my toes. As my body tingled, I returned the sensuous action. As the burning sun warmed our bodies, I placed his pole in my hand and soon caught the catch of my life!

Pate
- 1 lb halibut fillet
- 1 tablespoon lemon juice
- ½ cup white wine

Place the fish in a pot with the wine and lemon juice and poach for 10 minutes. Remove from the liquid and let it cool. Reserve the poaching liquid

Spread
- 4 oz. goat cheese
- 1 teaspoon poaching broth
- 1 garlic clove mince

- 2 teaspoons fresh lemon juice

Place the cheese, broth, and garlic in a processor. Pulse four times. Add the cooled halibut and the lemon juice and process until smooth. Spoon into the hallowed-out lemon cups and garnish with a sprig of curly leaf parsley. *Serves 4*

Lemon Cups:
Cut the tips from a lemon so they sit flat without tipping. Cut a zigzag pattern in the center of each lemon, cutting through the middle. Gently break apart the shell. Juice each half and reserve the juice for later use. With the tip of a sharp knife, remove as much of the inside as possible. Fill with the pate.

Charismatic Clams Fire Island

One of my greatest joys while living on Fire Island was navigating my dingy around the Great South Bay to receive gunny sacks full of clams from one of many "shallow water sailors" Approaching their boat, I excitedly and dreamily wished I would see my stranger dropping anchor. Handing me a sack, our hands would brush against one another's. His touch would be powerful, his look tender. Showing me how to open clams would be thrilling. Coming towards me from behind, he would wrap his strong arms around mine and position my hands in his. He would then place the clam tool delicately between my fingers while I held the clam in the palm of my hand. I would feel his warm breath on the back of my neck as he now offered me his "gifts from the sea." Since I wanted my officer to be a gentleman, I teasingly held his tool, being careful to swallow the sweet juice dripping from the end. Festively finishing a meal of fresh clams, he always told me mine was the best!

Stuffing
- 1 dozen cherrystone clams
- 2 tablespoons Parmesan cheese
- 2 smashed garlic toes
- 4 diced shallots
- ½ cup seasoned bread crumbs
- 3 tablespoons butter
- 2 tablespoon chopped parsley
- red pepper flakes to taste
- 1 beaten egg
- 3 cloves minced garlic

- 1 teaspoon fresh lemon juice

Place the washed and scrubbed clams in a pot with about three inches of water and two smashed garlic cloves. Bring to a boil and steam until the shells open, about 20 minutes. Remove from the heat. Discard any unopened clams. Reserve the remaining shells. Discard the liquid. With a clam knife or sharp knife, remove the clams from the shell by placing the tip of the knife between the clam meat and the bottom of the shell. Place the clams on a cutting board and chop fine. Place the clams in a bowl. Melt the butter in a pan and sauté the shallots. Add the garlic and red pepper flakes and cook for about 30 seconds. Add this to the bowl of clams. Add the breadcrumbs, parsley, lemon juice, cheese, and beaten egg. Combine thoroughly. Grease each shell with the remaining butter and place a rounded spoon of the stuffing on each half. Bake in a 350-degree oven for ten to fifteen minutes or until the clam mixture begins to form a light crust on the top. *Makes one dozen clams.*

Dreamy Floating Prawns in Artichoke Bottom Boats

Visualizing sitting down to our first dinner through my flight of imagination, seeing us beginning to strip the leaves of our artichoke in search of a soft, tender heart, left me panting. With each gentle tug of the leaf, we would sense our passion heightening. Looking across the table, he would begin to follow me with his bedroom eyes, seducing me in the same gentle manner as he had handled the leaves. As the candlelight reflected off my near-naked skin, he would lovingly blow me a kiss. His soft full lips gently opened as he moved to my side of the table, revealing

his moist tongue, which he began to run up and down the length of my neck. The search for the robust bottom was finally over.

- 2 tablespoons red bell pepper
- ½ cup cream
- 1 tablespoon minced white onion
- 1 tablespoon lemon juice
- 1 tablespoon butter
- 1 tablespoon capers
- 1 tablespoon flour
- ¼ lb. prawns 21-25 count
- 1 jar artichoke bottoms

Sauté the pepper and onion in the butter until the vegetables are tender. Sprinkle the flour on top and cook for about 1 minute, stirring continually. Gradually add the cream and lemon juice. Cook over medium-low heat until the mixture thickens. Peel, wash, and de-vein the prawns, and pat dry. Place in the hot cream mixture and cook for about one minute until they turn pink. Remove from the heat and add the capers. Place the artichoke bottoms on a platter lined with cooked artichoke leaves. Place a prawn inside each artichoke bottom. Drizzle sauce over the top.
Serves 2

Red Hot Salmon Cakes with Fresh Pineapple Salsa

Wishing he could be my date for the annual Mardi Gras party; with everyone in disguise, I could feel sumptuous being playful. The deep, purple, and brilliant green beads adoring my neck and dangling halfway down my bare chest, I gingerly lifted them to my mouth and lightly rolled them around my tongue, all the while seductively smiling at him. Placing a morsel of pineapple in his mouth and letting the beads quickly fall, I excitedly pressed my lips onto his and took the pineapple from his mouth with my quick darting tongue. Plucking a feather from my jewel-laden eye mask and calmly running it around the edges of his face, I repeated the pineapple scenario, adding some crushed red peppers for a more sweltering flavor. Wrapping his hands around my hanging beads, he leads me to a more private part of the house. I let my honey stir my firestorm even more!

Salmon Cakes
- 1 lb salmon filet washed and patted dry
- 1 tablespoon chopped jalapeno chili
- 2 tablespoons finely diced white onion
- 1 tablespoon finely diced red and yellow pepper
- 2 tablespoons cilantro finely chopped
- Juice of 1 lime
- 1 beaten egg
- 1 teaspoon salt

Bake the salmon filet at 375 degrees for 10 minutes. Remove from the oven and let the salmon cool. Flake the salmon into a

bowl. Add the remaining ingredients and, using your hands, mix until thoroughly combined. Shape into 4 round salmon cakes. Set aside.

Dredging Mixture
- ¼ cup flour
- 1 beaten egg
- 1 tablespoon lime juice
- 1 cup Japanese breadcrumbs
- 3 tablespoons melted butter

Place the flour on a plate. Lightly dredge the salmon cakes on both sides with the flour. Beat the egg and lime juice in a bowl large enough to hold each salmon cake. Dip the salmon cakes in the egg mixture, removing any excess liquid. Place the breadcrumbs on a plate. Coat each salmon cake in the breadcrumbs. Brown the salmon cakes in the melted butter over medium until golden.

Pineapple Salsa
- ½ fresh pineapple
- ¼ finely chopped red bell pepper
- Juice of 1 lime
- 1 thinly sliced green onion
- ¼ cup minced cilantro
- Dash red pepper flakes

Remove the rind from the pineapple. Cut the pineapple in half. Cut out the hard core that goes down the center of the pineapple half. Dice the pineapple. Place the pineapple with its juice into a bowl. Add the red bell pepper, green onion, cilantro, and lime juice. Stir until thoroughly combined. Chill 1 hour and serve with salmon cakes. *Makes 2 cups*

Spinach for My Baby & Chevre Stuffed Mushrooms

I can't seem to keep my mind from always wandering to him. Everything I see and touch somehow ends up with a fantasy story. As I stuffed these mushrooms, I was preparing myself for what some tender caresses from him would feel like. Barely closing my eyes and placing a daisy in the center of my yellow lace lingerie, I run my fingertips over and around the mounds. Feeling his head lightly pressing against my chest as he bent over to sniff the flower, he lowered the straps from my shoulders with his teeth. This brought a low guttural moan from deep within me.

Tenderly brushing over my upper body with his soft go-tee, he removed the daisy with his mouth and devoured my mushrooms!

Stuffing
- 4 large stuffing mushrooms caps removed
- salt and pepper to taste
- 2 tablespoons olive oil
- juice of a lemon
- ½ diced white onion
- ¼ cup pine nuts
- 2 minced garlic toes
- *¼ cup garlic croutons breadcrumbs
- 1 bunch fresh spinach
- 2 oz Chevre cheese
- 8 oz cream cheese softened

Using a wet paper towel, wipe the outside of the mushroom caps. Heat the olive oil in a pan, add the onions and garlic, and sauté until soft. Wash and coarsely chop the fresh spinach. Spin dry. Add to the onion mixture and stir with a spoon until wilted. Add the lemon juice stirring again. Season the mixture with salt and pepper and blend all the ingredients. Remove from the heat. Fold in the pine nuts and breadcrumbs. Set aside to cool. Crumble and add the Chevre cheese to the spinach mixture. Fold in the cream cheese until thoroughly combined. Stuff each mushroom cap with the spinach mixture and bake at 375 degrees until heated through about twenty minutes. *Serves 4*

*Garlic Croutons:
- 2 slices of sourdough bread
- 2 tablespoons butter
- 2 cloves minced garlic

Combine the butter and garlic. Spread the mixture on one side of the sourdough bread and broil until brown and bubbly. Allow bread to cool and harden. Then cut into croutons. Process the croutons until crumbs form.

Stimulating Skewered Hoisin Breast of Chicken with Peanut Dipping Sauce

Thinking this could be a great starter for our Chinese New Year celebration, I dipped the flesh into the peanut sauce and slowly nibbled the meat. This caused a fiery sensation in my mouth as the explosion went off. I only hoped we would have an opportunity to feed one another this arousing concoction and keep the explosions coming and coming.

Chicken
- 2 whole chicken breasts washed and patted dry
- 1 teaspoon sesame seeds
- ½ cup catsup
- 1 tablespoon soy sauce
- 2 tablespoons brown sugar
- 1 star anise grated
- 2 tablespoons Hoisin sauce
- 1 tablespoon rice vinegar

Combine all of the ingredients except for the chicken. Place the chicken in the marinade and refrigerate overnight, turning once. Remove the chicken from the marinade and cut it into half-inch strips. Soak 24 wooden skewers in water for 1 hour. Thread the chicken onto each skewer and grill or broil for three to five minutes per side. Serve with dipping sauce. *Serves 4*

Dipping Sauce:
- 3 green onions reserve green stems
- 4 tablespoons sesame oil
- 2 cloves garlic
- ¼ teaspoon five-spice
- 1-inch peeled ginger
- 1 tablespoon sugar
- 2 cups peanuts
- 3 tablespoons coconut milk
- 2 tablespoons seasoned rice vinegar
- 2 tablespoons soy sauce
- 2 tablespoons chopped peanuts
- green onion stems sliced thin

Mince the white part of the green onions, garlic, and ginger in a processor. Add all the other ingredients except the green onion stems and chopped peanuts and process until smooth. Remove from the processor bowl and pour into a dipping bowl. Sprinkle with the chopped peanuts and thin slices of the green onion stems.
Makes 2 cups

Fierce & Fiery Chicken Curry Empanadas with Coconut, Peanut, & Raisin Dipping Sauce

I now knew I was on a quest to find him. My yearning for the taste of him, the touch of him, the scent of him, the sound, and the sight of him arouses me. I could no longer contain my needs for him. Fierce and fiery would certainly describe what I

anticipated our affair to be. My mouth was not the only thing that needed cooling off!

Pastry
- 2 cups flour
- 1½ cubes butter
- ¼ teaspoon cayenne
- ¼ teaspoon ground cumin
- ¼ teaspoon ground coriander
- 1 teaspoon salt
- 1/3 cup cold Mexican beer

Place the flour, butter, salt, and spices in the bowl of a processor and process until coarsely chopped. Pour the beer through the feed tube and continue to process until the dough forms a ball around the processor bowl. Remove the dough from the bowl and wrap it in plastic wrap. Refrigerate for 1 hour. On a floured surface, roll the dough into a 9x12 rectangle. Using a 3-inch round cookie cutter, cut out twelve circles. Stack circles between layers of plastic wrap and refrigerate until ready to use. *Makes 12 shells*

Curry Paste
- 1 whole dried chili
- ¼ cup chopped white onion
- 4 chopped garlic cloves
- 2 teaspoons lime zest
- 2 teaspoons ground coriander
- ¼ teaspoon cardamom
- ¼ teaspoon cumin
- ½ teaspoon cinnamon
- 1 tablespoon chili oil

Place the chili in warm water to cover and let it soak until soft for about 1 hour. Drain the chili and remove the seeds. Place in a processor with the remaining ingredients process until smooth. *Makes about ¼ cup*

Chicken Curry
- 1 tablespoon chili oil
- 1 teaspoon salt
- 2 whole chicken breasts washed, dried, and cut into ¼-inch chunks
- 2 tablespoons curry paste
- 8 oz cream cheese

Heat the chili oil in a pan. Sauté the chicken chunks until cooked. Season the chicken with salt. Add the curry paste and stir until the chicken is coated. Remove from the heat and let it cool. *Makes 2 cups*

Combine the cooked chicken with the cream cheese and place a tablespoon of this mixture into the center of each empanada round. Moisten the edge with water and fold the dough over the filling to form a half-circle. Close with the tines of a fork. Bake 450 degrees on an un-greased baking sheet for approximately fifteen minutes. Brush the tops with an egg glaze before baking.

Egg Glaze
- 1 egg beaten with 1 tablespoon of cream

Santa Fe Chutney
- 1 lb pippin apples cored and cut into chunks
- 1 cup apple cider vinegar
- 1 lb Santa Rosa plums pits removed and cut into quarters
- 1 chopped red onion

- ¼ lb white sugar
- 3 cloves garlic minced
- ¼ lb brown sugar
- 2 whole cinnamon sticks
- 1 inch piece ginger peeled and grated
- 1 teaspoon fresh cloves
- ½ teaspoon cumin seed
- 1 teaspoon salt
- ¼ lb white raisins
- ¼ lb dark raisins

Place all the ingredients into a large pot. Bring to a boil. Reduce heat and simmer for about one hour until the mixture is thick and most of the liquid has evaporated. During the cooking process, if the mixture looks too dry, add ½ cup of apple cider. *Makes about 1 quart*

Dipping Sauce:
Combine 1 cup chutney with ¼ cup Spanish peanuts and ¼ cup fresh grated coconut. *Makes about 1 1/2 cups*

Aphrodisiac Chicken Breast, Artichoke Heart & Feta Satchels Tied with Leek Bows

With the heat from the crackling fire, our favorite New Age artist playing in the background, and another bottle of wine just opened, I felt the tingling and cloudy effects of this combination awaken feelings of my desire for him. Wondering what kinds of things he might contemplate looking at the stuffed, tied chicken, my thoughts were interrupted watching him remove his tie and bind my wrists. Ordering me to close my eyes and open my mouth, he set in motion the task of placing different foods into my mouth, one right after the other. Feeling the overflow dribbling down my chin and onto my neck stimulated my wanting something hot and sticky. The packet he soon gave me filled this desire.

Satchels
- 1 lb chicken breast
- 2 tablespoons roasted red peppers
- 2 cloves garlic
- 6 oz artichoke hearts
- 2 tablespoons olive oil
- 3 oz feta cheese
- Salt & pepper to taste
- 10 Kalamata olives
- 2 tablespoons sun-dried tomato
- 1 package puffed pastry

Cut the chicken breast into chunks and place it in a processor bowl. Pulse 3-4 times. Heat the olive oil in a pan. Add the garlic cloves and cook for 10 seconds. Remove the cloves from the pan.

Add the cut-up chicken breasts and season with salt and pepper to taste. Sauté until the chicken is cooked. Remove from the heat and place into a bowl. Dice the sun-dried tomatoes and roasted red peppers. Add to the chicken. Julienne the artichoke hearts, crumble the Feta and add to the chicken mixture. Cut the Kalamata olives in half and add them to the chicken mixture. Mix all ingredients until thoroughly combined. Cut each sheet of puffed pastry into six 3-inch squares. Place a heaping tablespoon of the chicken mixture into the center of each square. Gather the four corners over the top of the filling and squeeze it shut. Tie with leek bows and bake at 425 degrees for about 20 minutes or until puffy and golden brown. *Makes 12*

Leek Bows
One leek

Remove the first layer of skin from the leek. Wash the leek under cold running water. Cut away the white part from the green part. Reserve the white part for later use. Plunge the green stems into boiling water. When wilted, remove from the boiling water with a slotted spoon and plunge into a bowl of ice water. When cooled, remove from the bowl and pat dry. Cut leeks into 12 strands. Tie around satchels to form a bow.

CHAPTER TWO
WARM-HEARTED AFFAIR
Soup

Looking down Beaver Creek, I spotted him atop the rocks reading Thoreau as the cool, rushing water caressed his feet. Sensuous soups prepared to warm his soul and rouse his body was offered in kettles and crocks along the creek side as I introduced myself to him!

Sumptuous Shrimp Bisque with Prawn Sauté

The soft patter of rain on the roof and the crackling of the robust fire set the stage for romance on our first date. Nibbling my neck as I stripped the shrimp from their shell, he began to set the stage for an intimate evening. Stripping off my sweater, he began to stretch it over my head without totally removing it. Spinning me around, he continued his masterful art of nibbling until he reached my waist. Then he spun me back around and repositioned my sweater. I decided to let his passion simmer along with this soup.

- 1½ lb (16 to 20) shrimp
- 2 cups chicken stock
- 2 toes garlic
- 1 sliced onion
- 2 cups celery with leaves
- 3 stems of parsley
- 1 bay leaf
- 1 teaspoon peppercorns
- 1 teaspoon salt and pepper

Peel the shrimp setting 6 aside with their tails intact. De-vein shrimp, wash and let drain in a colander. In a medium-size pot, place the shrimp shells and the remaining ingredients. Simmer for 20 minutes. Strain the stock, saving the liquid and disposing of the solids. Set aside.

- ½ cup butter
- 2 cups cream
- pinch paprika
- ¼ cup flour
- reserved stock
- ¼ cup chopped dill

In the same pan, melt the butter. Add the shrimp with their tails intact and sauté. Season the shrimp with salt, pepper, and garlic. Remove and set aside. Coarsely dice the remaining shrimp and add to the butter. Cook until pink. Remove from the pan and set aside. Sprinkle the flour over the butter and make a roux. Cook constantly stirring for 2 to 3 minutes, making sure the roux does not brown. Gradually add the reserved stock and cook until thick. Gradually add the cream, stirring until thoroughly heated. Season the soup with salt, pepper, a pinch of paprika, and dry sherry. Add the cooked shrimp. Ladle into warm bowls and float a sauté prawn with tail intact in the middle of the soup. Sprinkle dill on top.
Serves 4 to 6

Luscious Lip Licking Cream of Smoked Salmon Soup with Dill Crouton

The gentle rhythm of the rocking boat mesmerized our gaze as the spectacular sunset over the horizon. Handing him a mug of steamy soup, he brought it towards his salmon-colored lips. The instant his lips tasted this wonderful soup, he wanted to taste mine. Placing one hand behind my neck and the other on my hips, he pulled me closer to him. I could feel his rising desire intensify with each movement of the waves. Laying me against the stiff and hard rope, I wrapped my arms around him and held on tight. At that point, the salmon wasn't the only thing that was smoking!

Dill Crouton
- ½ loaf French bread
- ½ cube melted butter
- 1 teaspoon garlic powder
- 2 tablespoons dried dill

Cut the bread into 8 equal slices. Brush with the melted butter. Season the bread with garlic and dill. Broil both sides until golden brown. Set aside

Smoked Salmon Soup
- ½ cube butter
- 2 tablespoons flour
- ½ lb smoked salmon
- 1 white onion diced
- 3 cups half & half
- 2 tablespoons lemon juice

- 4 toes garlic minced
- 8 oz cream cheese

Melt the butter in a large pot. Over medium-low heat, sauté the onion and garlic until soft. Sprinkle the flour over the onion and cook, constantly stirring, for 2 minutes. Gradually add the 3 cups of half & half and cook until the liquid coats the back of a spoon. Break the cream cheese into pieces and drop them into the soup. Reduce flame to low and stir until the cream cheese is thoroughly combined into the soup. Cut away 3 ounces of the smoked salmon and set it aside. Puree the remaining salmon in a food processor. Add the pureed salmon to the soup and stir well to combine. Add the lemon juice to the soup. Stir and ladle the hot soup into bowls. Equally, divide the reserved salmon and sprinkle it over the hot soup. Place a dill crouton in the middle of the soup. *Serves 6 to 8*

Brazen Braised Beef & Vegetable Soup with Herb Dumplings

This particular soup was fashioned during the winter my beau and I were snowbound at my cabin on the lake. While mixing the dumplings, he entered the kitchen and suggested that he help me. With the front of his body against the back of mine, he slipped his arms on the sides of my waist and into the bowl of dough. He grasped my hands and held them in his, and we began to knead the dough in a rhythmic pattern. Using his tongue, he traced the outsides of my earlobes every now and then, plunging his tongue deep into my ear. As the snowfall built, we created our own personal storm as this soup bubbled in a cast iron pot over the fire.

- 3 lbs beef soup bones
- 2 lbs chuck roast
- 1 lb baby carrots
- 2 lbs creamers cut in half
- 1 bunch diced celery
- 1 large white diced onion
- 1 tablespoon garlic powder
- 1 tablespoon dried thyme
- 1 tablespoon dried marjoram
- 2 tablespoons tomato paste
- 2 parsnips cut into ¼ inch pieces

The day before making the soup, season the beef bones and chuck roast with salt, pepper, and garlic powder. Roast at 375 degrees for 3 hours. Remove from the oven and allow the beef to cool. Chill. The next day place the beef bones in a large pot and cover them with water. Bring to a boil, reduce the heat and simmer for 3 hours, making sure that the water level does not get below the bones. Remove the bones from the broth and add the chuck roast that has been cut into ½-inch chunks. Cook for 1 hour. Add the remaining vegetables and herbs and cook for 30 minutes over medium-low heat. When the vegetables are tender, add the dumplings. *Serves 8*

Dumplings
- 1 cup cake flour
- ½ teaspoon salt
- egg
- ½ teaspoon garlic powder
- 2 tablespoons chopped parsley
- milk
- 2 teaspoons baking powder
- 2 tablespoons Parmesan cheese

Mix the dry ingredients in a bowl and set aside. Add the parsley and Parmesan cheese. Break the egg into a 1 cup measuring cup and fill with milk until the cup is ½ full. Beat well and slowly pour the liquid into the dry ingredients. Using a fork, mix the ingredients until thoroughly combined. Add more milk if the batter is too stiff. Dip a teaspoon into hot water, then dip the spoon into the batter. Drop the batter into the stock. Repeat until all the dumpling batter is gone. Simmer uncovered for 5 minutes. Turn and simmer 5 minutes longer.

Memories are Made of This Sweet Yellow Tomato Soup with Crème Fraiche & Black Caviar

The sultry flavor of this soup could only be enhanced when it was shared with my loved one on a stifling summer evening. Sitting closely on the verandah and listening to the sounds of crickets and cicadas chirping and watching fireflies flit across the pond, I then suggested we go in for a cool shower. Before I knew it, he was at my side. Unbuttoning my clammy and sticky blouse, he began to sponge me with cool water scented with lavender. Stepping out of my hip huggers, he continued to bathe me. I returned the cool favor. Positioning ourselves on the cushioned bamboo fainting couch, we felt it was time for the insects to listen to our music. To finish, we toasted to the end of another wonderful summer spent together enjoying the simple things in life.

- 4 lbs. coarsely chopped yellow tomatoes
- 1 cup chicken stock
- ½ cup diced red onions
- 2 cloves minced garlic
- ¼ cup chopped fresh parsley
- ¼ cup julienne basil leaves
- 1 cup sliced celery with leaves
- Salt and pepper to taste

Place all ingredients in a pot. Bring to a boil. Lower the heat and simmer for 30 minutes. Remove from the heat and allow the

mixture to cool. Puree the soup in a food processor. Salt and pepper the soup to taste. Chill

Crème Fraiche & Black Caviar
- 1 cup heavy cream
- 1 cup sour cream

Mix the cream and sour cream in a bowl until thoroughly combined. Cover and let stand in a warm place for 12 hours until the mixture thickens. Remove the cover and stir well. Refrigerate for a day and a half before using.
   1container of black caviar
   4 sprigs of Italian parsley

Ladle the soup into chilled bowls and place a tablespoon of crème Fraiche in the center of the soup. Place 1 teaspoon of caviar on top of the crème Fraiche. Garnish with a sprig of parsley.
Serves 4

Come Kiss Me Lemon Soup with Parsley Pasta & Roasted Chicken Julienne

One lemony taste of this soup made him pucker up for some of my erotic kisses! His full wet lips, so soft and tender, sent chills up and down my spine. Kissing his eyelids, nose, ears, chin, and jaw only energized me to continue. Circling his pecs with my tongue was thrilling! Rubbing lemon oil on the insides of his thighs accompanied by pronounced kisses made him keenly aware of what would happen next. Flitting my tongue between his toes and taking them into my awaiting mouth, soothingly sucking them, brought me back to the place I had started. And when we

finished tasting each other's lips, we discovered that this soup was also good served at room temperature.

- 8 cups chicken broth
- 2 tablespoons capers
- 2 tablespoon chopped parsley
- Juice of 2 fresh lemons
- zest of 1 lemon
- 3 egg yolks
- salt and cracked pepper to taste

Place the stock in a pot and heat. Beat the egg yolks and lemon juice together. Add ½ cup of the hot stock and whisk until thoroughly combined. Add this mixture to the soup. Increase the heat to medium, constantly stirring until the soup is very hot. Do not let the soup boil. Add the zest, capers, parsley, chicken, and pasta.

Parsley Pasta
- ¾ cup all-purpose flour
- 1 tablespoon lemon juice
- 1 teaspoon olive oil
- ¾ cups semolina flour
- 2 beaten eggs
- ½ teaspoon salt
- 1 teaspoon lemon pepper
- 2 tablespoons parsley
- water

Mix lemon pepper with the flours. Place on a cutting board, making a well in the center. Beat the lemon juice into the eggs and add the parsley. Pour the egg mixture into the center of the well.

Blend with a fork until thoroughly combined if the dough is too stiff, add a little more lemon juice one tablespoon at a time. If the dough is too wet, add more semolina flour, 1 tablespoon at a time. Knead in a pasta machine or by hand for 10 to 12 minutes. Roll the dough out very thin. Cut into the desired shape by hand or with a machine. Bring a pot of water to a boil; add 1 teaspoon of olive oil and ½ teaspoon of salt. Add the pasta. Cook for 3 to 5 minutes. Drain the noodle and add them to the soup.

Roasted Chicken Julienne
- 3 lb chicken
- 1 bunch rosemary stemmed
- 3 lemons
- 3 toes garlic
- 1 tablespoon lemon zest
- 1 bunch parsley
- ½ cube butter
- 1 tablespoon lemon juice
- Salt
- cracked pepper

Wash the chicken inside and out and pat dry. Cut the lemon into quarters and place it into the cavity with the fresh rosemary stem, a bunch of parsley, and peeled garlic. Mix the butter, lemon juice, and lemon zest into a bowl. Be careful not to tear the skin, gently separate the skin from the meat by inserting your index and middle finger between the meat and skin. Go as far back over the breast as you can without ripping the skin. Divide the butter mixture in half. Place the butter mixture under the skin of each breast area. Season the entire chicken with salt, cracked pepper, and garlic powder. Roast at 375 degrees for 60 to 75 minutes. Remove from the oven and let cool. Cut meat into julienne strips and add to the soup. *Serves 8*

Ti' Amo Mexicali Turkey Soup with Chili Lime Tortillas

Flamingo dancing, pitchers of Sangrias, and strumming guitars set the tone for our last Cinco De Mayo party, as my hombre and I made our own beautiful music. With our hands barely touching, our hearts pressed tightly together, and our eyes closed, we danced to the salsa music. I felt him release my comb as my hair fell softly over my shoulders. The darkness of my mind was fixated on enjoying this passionate scenario. I felt the cool liquid turn warm as he dipped the Sangria onto my hot and erect buds. Placing the headphones over my ears, he laid me back onto the colorful poncho that lay over the hearth of the fireplace. He unbuckled the ankle straps of my stilettos and began to caress my feet. As he worked his way up my body, my head was swimming from the Latin music and his touch. He bound my hands with the nylon strings of his Flamingo guitar ever so gently. Later we indulged in this superb soup to create a lasting lusty memory of that night!

- ¼ cup vegetable oil
- 4 toes minced garlic
- 2 fresh tomatoes diced
- 4 ribs thinly sliced celery
- 3 quarts of turkey broth
- 2 Anaheim chilies diced
- 2 ears white corn kernels removed
- 1 jalapeno pepper seeded and minced (optional)
- 1 tablespoon dried oregano
- 1 diced white onion

- 1 cup cooked black beans
- 1 diced red bell pepper
- 4 cups cooked diced turkey breast
- Salt and pepper to taste
- bunch cilantro
- ¼ cup lime juice

Heat the vegetable oil in a large pot. Add the garlic, onion, peppers, celery, and sauté until soft. Add the tomatoes and stir. Add the turkey broth. Add the corn kernels, salt and pepper, and oregano. Stir to combine the ingredients. Cook over medium heat for 5 minutes. Add the black beans, turkey, and cilantro. Stir and continue to cook until the soup is hot. Pour the lime juice into the soup and stir again. Ladle into a bowl and sprinkle with chili lime tortillas.

Chili Lime Tortillas
- 8 corn tortillas sliced into ¼ inch strips
- 1 tablespoon lime juice
- ¼ cup vegetable oil
- 2 teaspoon chili powder and salt mixed

Oil a cookie sheet. Toss the tortilla strips in a bowl with the oil and lime juice. Place the strips on the cookie sheet and bake at a preheated 400 degrees until golden brown and crisp, about ten minutes. Stir after five minutes. Remove from the oven and sprinkle with the salt mixture. Using your hands, toss the tortilla chips in the pan to make sure they are seasoned. Sprinkle over soup. *Serves 8*

More than Memorable Creamy Asparagus Soup with Crab

Strolling through the vegetable garden and sipping a mug of homegrown asparagus soup, my aficionado thrusts himself against me, trying to mimic the long, firm, meaty spears of asparagus pushing their way towards the sun. With spear in hand, I indulged as we frolicked through the vegetables in a

teasing way. We spent the remainder of the afternoon being very creative in our imitation of nature's bountiful harvest.

- 2 lbs fresh asparagus
- 1 cup half and half
- ½ lb. crabmeat
- 1½ quarts chicken stock
- 1 cup cream
- ¼ teaspoon saffron
- ½ teaspoon white pepper
- 1 stick butter
- ½ teaspoon lemon pepper
- 1 large leek
- salt to taste
- 4 tablespoons flour
- 2 teaspoons powdered garlic

Break off the tough ends of each asparagus spear. Bring a pot of water to a boil. Wash the asparagus spears and drop them into the boiling water. Cook for 3 minutes. Drain and place asparagus in a sink full of ice water. When thoroughly chilled, drain and set aside. Reserve 8 asparagus spears.

Measure ½ cup of chicken stock and place in a bowl. Add the saffron and let sit for 30 minutes.

Melt the butter over medium heat and sauté the leek. Sprinkle the flour over the leek and stir until all the flour is absorbed into the butter. Gradually add the saffron and the remaining chicken stock. Stir constantly.

Puree the asparagus in a food processor. Add the half and half and pulse 4 to 5 times. Add this mixture to the soup. Stir to combine the ingredients. Simmer for 20 minutes. Slowly add the cream to the soup. Season the soup with salt, pepper, and garlic powder. Ladle hot soup into a bowl and float a reserved asparagus spear on top. Divide the crab evenly into 8 portions and sprinkle over the soup. *Serves 8*

Soothing Chilled Avocado Soup with Cilantro Pesto

Among the throw pillows and strewn satin sheets, I set out a bamboo tray with chilled bowls and crisp white napkins, along with a frosted pitcher of ice-cold lemonade. Looking at his outstretched naked body and licking my lips, I sauntered towards the bed, only thinking of romping with him one more time. And, when my passion was satiated, then this cool-down soup was a must!

Avocado Soup
- 2 diced red bell peppers
- 1 jalapeno pepper seeded and diced
- 6 chopped ripe tomatoes
- ½ peeled & diced English cucumber
- 1 red onion chopped
- ¼ cup finely diced cilantro
- ¼ cup lime juice
- salt and pepper to taste
- 4 toes chopped garlic
- 2 cups tomato juice
- 1 teaspoon cumin powder
- 2 avocados mashed peeled and pitted
- 4 tablespoons sour cream

Place all of the ingredients except the avocado and tomato juice in a large bowl and combine well. Place half of these ingredients in a food processor and puree. Combine the puree with the remaining half. Gradually stir in the tomato juice.

Fold in the mashed avocado. Season and chill. Ladle soup into chilled bowls. Just before serving, place a tablespoon of sour cream and cilantro pesto on top of the soup. *Serves 4*

CHAPTER THREE
FLIRTY FIRSTS
Salad

Gazing over the luscious rows of organic greens, our eyes met as he tenderly brushed watercolor onto his canvas. Just as Monet painted in his garden, I would create artistic salads just for him.

Amorous Butter Leaf, Fresh Strawberry, Roasted Pecans & Blue Cheese Salad with Raspberry Vinaigrette

A spring picnic with my green-eyed lover was the raison d'être for devising this salad. Spreading the soft quilt onto the grassy knoll, I decided to concoct our meal at ground level. As we sat sipping strawberry margaritas, we took turns placing one berry in the bowl and then one in each of our mouths. He would twirl his tongue around the tips of my fingers and lick the lengths with a seductive twinkle in his eye. Refreshing our glasses, he bent down to kiss me. The combination of his sweet tongue and taste of the warm berry fired my desire. Kissing the sweet juice of the berry as it ran down his chin was just as tasty and moist as his supple lips.

- 2 heads Butter Leaf lettuce washed, dried, and torn into bite-size pieces
- 1 cup sliced fresh strawberries
- ½ cup roasted pecans
- ¼ lb crumbled Blue Cheese

Layer the above ingredients starting with the lettuce and ending with the cheese. Drizzle vinaigrette over the salad. *Serves 4*

Raspberry Vinaigrette
- ¼ cup raspberry vinaigrette
- 2 cloves of minced garlic
- cracked pepper and salt to taste
- ½ cup extra virgin olive oil
- 2 tablespoons fresh mint cut into julienne strips
- 1 tablespoon poppy seeds

Place all ingredients except the oil, poppy seeds, and mint in a processor and blend. Slowly drip the oil through the feed tube until all of the oil has been incorporated into the vinaigrette. Remove and place in a bowl. Fold in the mint and poppy seeds. *Makes one cup*

Splendor of Autumn Salad with Walnut Oil & Fig Vinaigrette

After my dark-hair god ravished me in the fallen pile of colorful leaves, I felt compelled to put together this invigorating salad hoping to "revisit" the leaves once again! The taste of the nut is my favorite.

- ½ lb. baby green spring mix
- 1 Asian pear cored stemmed and sliced into quarter-inch pieces
- ½ cup walnuts
- 4 oz. Roquefort Cheese
- 4 figs halved

Arrange the greens on four individual salad plates. Place a ¼ of the Asian pear atop each salad. Evenly sprinkle with the walnuts and Roquefort Cheese. Place two fig halves in the center and drizzle with the vinaigrette. *Serves 4*

Walnut Oil & Fig Vinaigrette
- ¼ cup fig vinegar
- 1 shallot
- 2 cloves garlic
- ¼ cup extra virgin olive oil
- 2 tablespoons walnut oil
- Cracked pepper and salt to taste

Place the above ingredients, except the oils, into the bowl of a process and process. Slowly add the oils through the feed tube until thoroughly combined. Season the vinaigrette with cracked pepper and salt. *Makes ¾ cup*

Blissful Baby Spinach Salad with Peppered Bacon Wrapped Dates & Creamy Feta Dressing

Since the hotel only had one room left with a single bed, wrapping up my date was a pre requisite for the evening. Since he did not have much room to maneuver, I wanted to intensify his romantic behavior. Tickling him from head to toe with the stems of the spinach, well knowing I would get the roll-over prize

when the time was right. Smearing the Feta over my smooth flesh brought out submissiveness that surprised us both.

- 2 bunches baby spinach were washed, drained, and dried with stems removed
- ½ lb peppered bacon cut in half width-wise
- 12 pitted dates
- ¼ lb Feta Cheese crumbled
- ½ cup walnut pieces

Place the dates on a broiling pan and wrap with bacon. Secure with a toothpick and broil until bacon is crisp. Drain on a paper towel and let cool. Place the spinach in a bowl. Remove the toothpick from the bacon-wrapped dates and lay it on top of the spinach. Sprinkle with Feta Cheese and walnuts. *Serves 4*

Creamy Feta Dressing
- juice of 2 fresh lemons
- 4 cloves minced garlic
- 3 oz creamy garlic Feta Cheese
- ½ cup extra virgin olive oil
- cracked pepper and salt to taste

Place all ingredients except olive oil and cracked pepper in the bowl of a processor. Blend until all ingredients are combined. Slowly drip the olive oil into a feed tube until it has been absorbed in the dressing. Remove and place the dressing into a bowl and sprinkle with cracked pepper. Drizzle over salad. *Makes one cup*

Alluring Triple Red Salad with Red Wine Vinaigrette & Olive Crouton

I always made sure to ONLY wear my reddest of lipsticks and my deepest red nail polish when preparing this one. Pressing my un-blotted lips against him, I predictably leave a trail of red lips up and down his body. Could this be why he requested this salad so often?

- 1 head red leaf lettuce
- 1 pound beefsteak tomatoes
- 1 roasted red pepper

Place the above ingredients in a salad bowl. Place croutons on top of the salad and drizzle on the vinaigrette. Serves 4

Olive Crouton
- ½ loaf long sourdough bread cut into ten slices
- 1 cup Kalamata olives puree
- ¼ cup Kalamata olive oil
- 1 tablespoon of dried parsley & garlic powder
- ¼ teaspoon salt & pepper

Brush the oil on each slice of bread. Season with salt, pepper, dried parsley, and garlic powder. Broil until golden brown. Remove from the broiler and spread with olive puree. Set aside. *Makes 10 slices*

Red Wine Vinaigrette
- ¼ cup red wine vinegar
- 1 tablespoon Dijon mustard
- 4 cloves minced garlic
- 2 tablespoons chopped parsley
- cracked pepper
- salt
- ½ cup Kalamata olive oil

Combine all the ingredients, except the oil, in the bowl of a processor and process until thoroughly blended. Place olive oil through the feed tube and continue to blend until the oil is absorbed in the dressing. *Makes ½ cup*

Dousing Tabouli

Saving some of the extra virgin olive oil from the salad being made, he came for a sample. I dipped the bread into the oil and rubbed it on his chest, arms and shoulders. He grabbed the bottle and picked me up. Carrying me upstairs, he placed me on the waterbed and began to undress me. He anointed my entire body and then poured the rest of the oil on top of the slippery mattress, working it in with his massive hands. We rode the waves, the oil

clung to our hair and body. Partaking in a sensuous body oil rub is our customary practice before we eat this salad.

- 2 heads curly leaf parsley
- ¼ cup lemon juice
- 1 head red leaf lettuce
- ½ cup extra virgin olive oil
- 1 bunch green onions
- 1 tablespoon allspice
- 1 Armenian cucumber
- 1 tablespoon of garlic powder
- 4 tomatoes
- salt & pepper to taste
- ½ cup fine-grain cracked wheat
- ¼ cup dried mint
- water

Place cracked wheat in a bowl with water to cover and soak until it expands to twice its size, about 10 minutes. Drain and set aside.

Wash the parsley, spin it dry, and place the parsley in the bowl of a processor. Pulse three or four times until the parsley is finely chopped. Remove from the bowl and place into a salad bowl.

Core the red leaf lettuce, wash the leaves, and spin dry. Stack four leaves on top of one another and roll tightly. Using a sharp knife, cut into ¼ inch slices. Repeat until all of the lettuce is used. Add the lettuce to the parsley.

Finely chop the tomatoes and add to the above mixture.

Add the cracked wheat

Slice the green onions into ¼ inch pieces and add to the salad.

Cut an inch off from each end of the cucumber and dice the flesh very finely. Add to the salad.

Pour the lemon juice and extra virgin olive oil into the salad. Season the salad with a heaping tablespoon of allspice and garlic powder. Season the salad with salt and fine grain black pepper.

Crumble the mint between the palms of your hand and add to the above ingredients. Toss until the ingredients are combined.
Serves 8

Bubbles, Bangles, and Baby Leaf Lettuce with Warm Goat Cheese & Mustard Vinaigrette

This is a special salad for a very special night. Filling the tub with hot steamy water and rose oil, I serve this on Valentine's Day while soaking in a bath full of bubbles and rose petals with my one and only! With an array of dimly lit candles surrounding the tub and floor and reading the sexy messages written with lipstick on the steamy mirror, we both get the bang of our life when he presents me with yet, another bangle!

- 2 heads baby butter leaf lettuce washed and dried
- ¼ lb. goat cheese
- ¼ cup seasoned breadcrumbs

Cut the goat cheese into 1-inch squares. Place the breadcrumbs on a plate and roll the goat cheese in the crumbs. Place on a cookie sheet and bake in a 375-degree oven until the cheese is warm, about 10 minutes. Place the heads of lettuce on individual salad plates. Place warm goat cheese on top of lettuce and drizzle with vinaigrette. *Serves 2*

Mustard Vinaigrette
- ¼ cup sherry vinegar
- 1/3 cup extra virgin olive oil
- 1 teaspoon Dijon mustard
- zest of 1 lemon
- 2 tablespoons diced fresh flat-leaf parsley

Place all ingredients in a bowl and whisk until thoroughly combined. *Makes ¾ cup*

Medley of Golden Root & Red Beet Salad with Honey Mustard Dressing

Rubbing a little honey around the rim of his ear and across his lobe, I would ever so gently lick it off. Offering me the root was always a guarantee.

- Pound each red and yellow beet
- Aluminum foil

Individually wrap red and yellow beets in foil and place them on a baking sheet. Bake the beets in a 375-degree oven for 30 to 45 minutes or until thoroughly cooked. Remove from the oven and let cool. Remove the foil from the beet and the skin along with it. Slice the beets into quarter-inch slices and place in on a platter. Drizzle with vinaigrette. *Serves 4-6*

Honey Mustard Vinaigrette
- ¼ cup red wine vinegar
- 2 tablespoons honey and Dijon mustard
- ½ cup extra virgin olive oil

In a bowl, whisk all of the ingredients together and season with salt and cracked pepper. *Makes about one cup*

Hotter Than Hot Grilled Sweet Potato Salad with Lime Poppy Seed Dressing

It was a warm sultry summer night. His comments about my sweet potatoes being so firm and tasty as they peeked out from the cloth that was holding them up stirred the fire; I felt for him. The heat from the air and his breath on the nape of my neck were identical to the fire coming from the grill. HOT!

- 2 large sweet potatoes
- water
- 1 tablespoon olive oil mixed with ¼ teaspoon crumbled dried red chili peppers

Place the sweet potatoes in a pot covered with water. Simmer for 15 minutes or until the center is still firm. Remove and let cool. Skin the potatoes. Slice into quarter-inch pieces. Brush with the oil and grill for about 5 minutes on each side. Remove from the heat and set aside.

- 4 cups mixed greens
- Red bell pepper sliced into ¼ inch rings
- 4 green onions

Starting with the greens, place the peppers, green onions, and sweet potatoes on a platter. Drizzle with the dressing. Serves 4

Lime Poppy Seed Dressing
- 1 tablespoon poppy seeds
- Jalapeno pepper seeded and chopped
- 1 teaspoon grated, fresh garlic
- ¼ cup fresh lime juice
- ¼ cup fresh orange juice
- 1 tablespoon honey
- ¼ cup olive oil
- salt to taste

Place the dressing ingredients in a bowl and whisk together. Makes about one cup

Sexy Southwestern Salad with Salsa Vinaigrette

Ripping off the ankle straps of my red satin Stilettos stunned me as he threw them across the room! Sensuously caressing my calves and working his way up my leg, the saucy Latin music fades in the background as our kisses deepened. With our sounds of heavy breathing, he pulls me to the floor. He places his hands in the middle of my back and pulls me towards him. When we finished dancing the Salsa, I dropped to my knees and sampled his hot and spicy southwestern offering.

Salad
- 1 head red leaf lettuce
- 1 avocado sliced into 6 pieces
- 1/4 lb jicama sliced into ¼ inch strips
- 1 cup cooked black beans
- 2 tomatoes cut into 6 wedges
- 1 bunch thinly sliced green onions
- 1 bunch finely chopped cilantro
- ¼ lb grated white cheddar cheese

Wash, dry, and tear lettuce into bite-size pieces. Place in a bowl and add the remaining ingredients. Pour the vinaigrette over the top of the salad and toss. *Serves 6*

Salsa Vinaigrette
- 2 lbs fresh tomatoes washed and cored
- 1 bunch cilantro washed and dried
- 4 green onions
- juice of 1 lime
- ¼ cup olive oil
- 1 teaspoon hot pepper oil (optional)

Place all of the ingredients, except the oil(s), in the bowl of a food processor and pulse until chunky, about 3-4 times. Remove and place in a bowl. Add the olive oil and stir to blend. *Makes 2 cups*

CHAPTER FOUR
RISING DESIRES
Breads

And once again, I watched my beautiful, slender love kneeling amidst the dahlias, chrysanthemums, and zinnias, tenderly snipping their long graceful stalks. The butterflies, rhythmically stirring within my stomach, matched those flitting from flower to flower. As the smoke from the outside oven permeated the crisp fall air, I felt the heat rise within me.

Herb Focaccia for My Honey

Watching the yeast rise from a relaxed state to one of expansion sent my mind reeling. I could not wait for him to return. I dreamed of placing him between two slices of focaccia, nibbling until I got a rise out of him! YUM!

- 2 packages yeast
- 1 tablespoon sugar
- ½ cup warm water
- 2 tablespoons olive oil
- 8 cups unbleached flour
- 3 teaspoons salt
- 2 tablespoons chopped fresh garlic and parsley
- 2 cups warm water

Mix yeast and sugar. Dissolve in ½ cup of warm water. Set aside until bubbly, about 8 to 10 minutes. Add the olive oil. In another bowl, mix the flour, salt, parsley, and garlic. Add 2 cups of warm water and yeast mixture. Stir until thoroughly combined. Knead until smooth, about 10 minutes. Grease a large bowl with olive oil. Place dough in a bowl and turn once. Cover with plastic wrap and put in a warm place until it doubles in size, about one hour. Punch dough down. Place the dough on a well-oiled 12 x 18 baking sheet. Flatten to about a ½ inch thickness, pulling and stretching the dough until it fits the pan. Make indentations with your fingers.

TOPPING
- ¼-1/2 cup olive oil
- ¼ cup grated Parmesan Cheese
- 4 toes of minced garlic

Brush with olive oil. Sprinkle the garlic and Parmesan cheese on top. Bake at 400 degrees for 20 minutes. *Makes one sheet of focaccia bread.*

Three-Seeded Breadstick Hearts

Quite often, he caresses my heart and makes it pound! Now, I have found a way to return the feeling. I seductively twist the dough into forbidden forms and entice him to join me in a nibble. These risqué breadsticks are a must for an out-of-the-ordinary indulgence.

- 1 package yeast
- 1 tablespoon sugar
- 1 cup warm water
- 3 tablespoons olive oil

Place the yeast and sugar in a bowl and mix. Add the warm water and stir. Let stand for 8 to 10 minutes. Add the olive oil and stir again.

- 2 cups whole wheat flour
- 1 cup unbleached white flour
- ½ teaspoon salt
- 1 teaspoon garlic powder

Place the flours in a bowl. Add the salt and garlic powder and mix well. Pour the yeast mixture over this and combine well. Knead until the dough is soft and pulls away easily from the bowl, about 8 to 10 minutes. If the dough is too sticky, gradually add 2 to 4 tablespoons of unbleached flour.

Grease a large bowl. Place the dough in a bowl and turn once. Cover and put in a warm place (gas ovens are an excellent area for letting the dough rise). Let rise 1 hour. Punch down and knead about 4 to 6 times. Roll into a 6 x 9-inch rectangle. Cover and let

rise again for 30 minutes. Cut dough into 10 six-inch strips. *Makes 10 hearts*

- egg white
- ¼ cup each sesame, poppy, and cumin seeds mixed together

Brush strips with egg white and roll into seeds. Put ends together and form into heart shapes. Place on a greased baking pan. Bake 375 degrees, 25 to 30 minutes. Serve warm or allow the hearts to cool to room temperature. Store the hearts in airtight containers.

NOTE: The dough may be left in long strips and baked into bread strips.

Tipsey Kalamata Olive & Rosemary Bread

One of my favorite pleasures is to place these exotic pitted olives on the ends of my luscious tips and let him savor the taste one lick at a time.

- 1 package yeast
- 1 teaspoon sugar

- 1¾ cup warm water

Combine the yeast and sugar in a bowl. Add the water and mix until combined. Let the yeast sit until bubbly for 8 to 10 minutes.

- 5 cups bread flour
- 1 cup pitted Kalamata olives
- 1 tablespoon fresh rosemary

Place 2 cups of flour in a bowl. Add the yeast mixture and beat until a dough forms. Cover the dough and let sit for 20 minutes. Add the other 3 cups of flour, beating until the dough forms a soft ball. Add the rosemary and the Kalamata olives. Knead the herbs and olives into the dough.

- ¼ cup olive oil
- 1 bunch rosemary de-stemmed and divided in half

Mix the olive oil and rosemary in a deep bowl. Divide the dough into quarters. Divide each quarter into 6 pieces. Dip each piece into the rosemary oil. Shake off any excess oil. Place each piece into an oiled soufflé dish, sprinkling each layer with any remaining rosemary. Cover and let rise for 1 hour. Bake 350 degrees for one hour. Cool and serve. *Makes one loaf*

Tempting Tomato Bread for the Man of My Dreams

The love of my life has an obsession with hot tomatoes, which is unparallel to my love for him. He calls me his "Hot Tomato" as I tempt him with the juicy flesh that he squeezes between his firm, unyielding fingers.

- ¼ cup milk
- 5 cups of bread flour
- 2 packages yeast
- 2 sticks of salted butter cut into tablespoon portions
- 2 tablespoons sugar
- 2 cups drained sun-dried tomatoes packed in oil
- 6 beaten eggs

Place the milk in a saucepan and heat to lukewarm. (110 degrees) Remove from the heat and sprinkle in the yeast and sugar. Stir until dissolved. Blend in the eggs. Place in a large bowl and gradually add the flour until a smooth dough forms.

Gradually mix in the butter, cutting it into small pieces at a time. Place the dough in a mixing bowl and knead with a dough hook or by hand for 6 to 8 minutes. Remove dough from the bowl cover and refrigerate overnight. In the morning, punch the dough down and divide it into 2 equal pieces. Shape each piece into a rectangle.

Sprinkle 1 cup of sun-dried tomatoes over the top of each rectangle. Roll into a log folding the ends under. Place each loaf into a buttered loaf pan. Place in a warm spot and let rise until doubled in size, about 1 hour. Before baking the loaves, brush them with an egg wash. Bake in a preheated 375-degree oven for

about 30 minutes. Remove the loaves from the oven and cool.
Makes 2 loaves

EGG WASH:
- 1 egg
- 1 tablespoon cream

Thoroughly beat the egg with the cream.

Very "A-peeling" Roasted Garlic Yeast Bread

As he lay across the bedspread, fully clothed, advancing towards him, I begin to undo his belt. The sound of his zipper being released still did not entice him to open his eyes. Tonguing his belly button and kissing his tight stomach was abruptly halted when he placed his hands on my head and ran his fingers through

my soft hair. Peeling his pants off was as easy as peeling the skins off the roasted toes of garlic.

- 1 head garlic
- 1 package yeast
- 5 cups flour
- Olive oil
- 1 tablespoon sugar
- 1 cup warm water
- Salt
- ¼ cup of warm water

Cut off the top quarter of the head of garlic. Drizzle with olive oil and sprinkle with salt. Place in a 350-degree oven and bake until soft, about 20 minutes. Remove from the oven and let cool.

Combine the yeast and the sugar with ¼ cup of warm water. Stir and set aside until bubbly, about 10 minutes. In another bowl, add 5 cups of flour, the dissolved yeast mixture, and 1 cup of water. Beat until dough forms. Squeeze garlic toes from the roasted head of garlic and knead into the dough. Knead until smooth, about 10 minutes. Cover and let it sit for about 20 minutes. Grease a bowl with olive oil. Place the dough in a bowl and turn it once. Cover and let rise in a warm place until doubled 1 hour. Punch down and remove from the bowl. Form into a round ball or long loaf and place on an oiled baking sheet. Cover and place in a warm place for 30 minutes. Bake in a 350-degree oven for 45 minutes to one hour. *Makes one loaf*

Basil Pesto Bread to Fantasize About

Each summer, I fantasize about lying with him on a bed of basil that has been warmed by the morning sun. Rubbing his body with the oil from the leaves while lustfully licking his anatomy makes summer my favorite season! Imagine dripping and dipping the bread in a little hot basil oil and indulging in a powerful sampling of summer's preferential herb!

- ½ cup salted butter
- ½ cup sugar
- 2 cups half & half
- 2 beaten eggs

Mix the butter and sugar until well blended. Add the half & half and beaten eggs. Stir until well blended and set aside.

- 3 cups unbleached flour
- 2 cups whole wheat flour
- ½ cup grated Pecorino Cheese
- ¼ cup chopped fresh basil
- 1 cup pine nuts
- 1 teaspoon salt
- 2 tablespoons baking powder
- 2 tablespoons chopped Italian flat-leaf parsley
- 2 tablespoons minced garlic

In a large bowl, combine the flours, cheese, baking powder, herbs, garlic, pine nuts, and salt. Mix thoroughly. Add wet mixture to flour mixture and blend until all ingredients are moist.

Divide batter between 3 well-greased one-pound coffee cans filling them each halfway. Bake 350 degrees for 45 minutes. Cool in the cans. Remove the bread from the cans and wrap it airtight.
Makes 3 loaves

Soft & Soothing Yukon Gold Potato Buns

As we lay naked on the floor, thumbing through the stacks of travel brochures to the Yukon, I could not stop myself from kneading the soft, supple buns on my baby. Gently poking my fingers into his tender mass of flesh soon sent us traveling in another direction.

- 3 Yukon Gold potatoes washed and quartered
- water

Place potatoes in a pan covered with water, and cook until soft. Drain and reserve one cup of the potato water to keep it warm. Mash the potatoes. Set aside.

- 2 packages of dry yeast
- 2 teaspoons sugar

- ½ cup warm potato water

Mix the yeast and sugar in a bowl. Add the potato water. Stir and let sit for 8 to 10 minutes.

- 1¼ cups salted butter
- ½ cup potato water
- ½ cup honey
- 2 beaten eggs
- 6-7 cups flour

Heat salted butter and the remaining ½ cup of potato water in a pan until the butter has melted. Cool to lukewarm (110 degrees). Stir into the yeast mixture. Add ½ cup of honey, eggs, and mashed potatoes. Beat until well combined. Add 3 cups of flour and mix for 2 to 3 minutes. Gradually stir in 3 more cups of flour. The dough should hold together and leave the side of the bowl. If the dough is too sticky, gradually knead in one more cup of flour. Knead until dough is soft and pliable, about 8 to 10 minutes. Grease a large bowl. Place the dough in a bowl and turn once. Cover and let rise in a warm place until doubled (1 ½ hour). Punch down and knead 4 to 6 times to release any bubbles. Cut the dough into quarters. Divide each piece into 8 pieces. Shape into a smooth ball and place onto a greased baking pan. Cover and let rise until double in size, about 30 minutes. Bake 400 degrees for 20 to 25 minutes. *Makes 32 rolls.*

Sizzling Southwestern Coil Bread

This bread was shaped after my lover and I spent a hot sultry night on the Gulf. After quenching our thirst in the cantina, we lazily strolled on the beach hand in hand. Drawing images in the sand with our toes of our sexual desires was our method of communicating. The rule of our game was to complete the picture before the next wave rolled in and carried our sizzling scenario out to sea. The winner and the loser are exalted in the finale, never realizing there were so many ways to coil up.

- Combine in a large bowl and set aside.
- 2 ½ cups unbleached flour
- 2 packages dried yeast
- 1 tablespoon sugar and salt

Blend and heat in a saucepan over low heat until very warm. (120 degrees) Then add this to the flour mixture and stir well.

- ½ cup milk
- ¼ cup garlic oil
- 1 cup stale beer (measure beer and leave at room temperature overnight)

Mix until well moistened and beat for three minutes. Add to the flour mixture.

- 1 cup grated extra-sharp white cheddar cheese
- ¼ cup minced green chilies
- 1 tablespoon garlic powder

Stir in
- 3 ½-4 cups flour, which will make a sticky dough.

Gradually knead in:
- 1/3 – ½ cups more flour until dough is smooth and not sticky.

When the dough forms a smooth ball, place it into a greased bowl turning once. Cover and let rise in a warm place until double in size. Punch down dough. Divide the dough in half. Roll each half into a long rope. Grease a 9inch round cake pan. Place one end of the rope in the center of the pan and roll the rope into a small coil tucking the ends under. Repeat with the other rope. Cover and let rise for 30 minutes. Bake at 350 degrees for 35 to 45 minutes.

NOTE: If bread becomes too brown, cover with foil for the last 10 minutes

CHAPTER FIVE
SOMETHING ON THE SIDE
Side Dishes

My lover gifts me in a round clay bowl rosemary, basil, cilantro, and thyme. Plucking the tender herbs, I passionately prepare sensuous side dishes.

Sumptuous Syrian Rice

I serve this to him with only a rhinestone in my curviest naval, shimmering gold bracelets with a sheer chiffon scarf veiling all but my blazon brown eyes. An erotic belly dance brings me the crown jewel!

- 2 tablespoons butter
- 2 toes garlic minced
- 8 strands of vermicelli broke into 1-inch pieces
- 1 cup rice
- ½ cup pine nuts
- 2 cups chicken stock
- ¼ cup chopped parsley

Melt the butter in a saucepan. Add the vermicelli and stir until it is golden brown. Add the rice stirring to coat the grains. Add the chicken stock, pine nuts, and garlic. Stir again. Cover the saucepan and bring it to a boil. Reduce heat to medium-low and cook until rice is soft, 15 to 20 minutes. Turn the fire off and let it set for 5 minutes. Place rice in a bowl and garnish with fresh, chopped parsley. *Serves 3 to 4*

Soothing Couscous with Tomatoes & Fresh Mint

One balmy summer night, I made a bed of palm leaves on the sand. After lighting some votive candles, I pass a plate of dates, dried apricots, and figs. We listen to the soft sounds of the sea serenade us as we experience a Mediterranean evening. After

setting the scenario by sucking on a few anise seeds and sips of anise tea, he is ready to give me his Turkish delight.

- 2 cups chicken stock
- 2 diced tomatoes
- 4 toes minced garlic
- 1 cup fine grained couscous
- ½ cup chopped mint

Place the chicken stock in a saucepan and bring to a boil. Add the tomatoes and garlic and stir. Gradually add the couscous stirring well after each addition. As the liquid is absorbed, the couscous will expand. When the couscous is soft, remove it from the heat and stir in the fresh mint. *Serves 4*

Frolicking Risotto with Italian Parsley

Mounting his stallion, we ride like the wind. Pressing my bare chest against the hot skin of my aficionado, we embark on our fantasy. Swilling and swirling a full-bodied red wine after a long exhausting ride, we feast on this frolicking dish.

- 2 cups chicken stock
- 6 threads saffron
- ¼ cup butter
- 1 small diced white onion
- 1 cup risotto
- 3 cloves of minced garlic
- ¼ cup chopped Italian leaf parsley

Soak the saffron in the cold chicken stock about one hour before preparing the risotto. Melt the butter in a pan and sauté the onion until soft. Add the risotto and garlic, and stir to coat the ingredients. Add the chicken stock and stir again. Reduce heat to low, cover, and cook for 10 to 15 minutes until the risotto is soft, stirring every 5 minutes. If the risotto needs more liquid, add more chicken stock ¼ cup at a time. Fold in the chopped parsley and serve. *Serves 3 to 4*

Daring Dried Fruit & Wild Rice with Pineapple Thyme

Hiking through the grove of Aspen trees, brilliantly colored in hues of orange, yellow, and bright red, I spread our plaid tartan onto the ground near the creek's edge. The relaxing sound of the trickling water sets the mood for our fall picnic, which consisted of roast pheasant, red pear salad, and the following course. As we seductively feed one another, stopping for some languid kisses in between, we realize the heat from the campfire prompts us to engage in a more natural action for creating heat on these chilly autumn nights.

- 1 cup brown rice
- 2 cups water
- ½ cup wild rice

- 1¼ cups water
- ½ cup dried apricots sliced into ¼ inch pieces
- ¼ cup dried cranberries
- zest and juice of an orange
- 4 green onions sliced thin
- ¾ cup chopped pecans
- 1 tablespoon fresh pineapple thyme leaves

Place two cups of water in a pot and bring to a boil. Add the brown rice. Cover and reduce heat to low and simmer for about 45 minutes or until rice is soft. Place the wild rice in another pan with 1 ¼ cups of boiling water. Cover and reduce heat, simmering until rice is tender, about 30-45 minutes. When the rices are cooked, place them in a bowl with the remaining ingredients. This dish can be served warm or at room temperature. *Serves 5-6*

Heavenly Angel Hair Pasta with Lemon Butter & Chervil

Lying beneath the stars on the cool grass, we search the heavens for Celestial beings. With our cheeks lightly touching, I can feel the prickles from his five o'clock shadow brush against my tender skin. The fragrance of his cologne causes my eyelids to fall to half-mast as I take him in through all my senses. Without opening my eyes, I feel him place me upon his rocket as we float through space. I know we have climbed the stairway to heaven.

- 1 lb angle hair pasta cooked, rinsed, drained, and kept warm
- 2 cubes salted butter
- ¼ cup fresh lemon juice
- zest of 1 lemon
- 6 toes minced garlic
- 1 bunch finely chopped chervil
- 2 oz. Parmesan cheese

Melt butter in a saucepan over low heat. Add the lemon juice, lemon zest, garlic, and chervil. Pour over pasta and toss to coat. Grate fresh Parmesan over the top. *Serves 6.*

Fettuccine with Sun-Dried Hot Tomato Oil

Canoeing on a Sunday afternoon can be a most enjoyable caper. I pack the lunch, and he picks the place. Gliding around the pond and throwing bread to the ducks as the warm breeze hugged the air, we deviated from our usual course. Before we knew it, we were at the edge of a beautiful meadow bursting with wildflowers. Carrying me from the canoe and laying me down in the colorful field, he picks deep purple Lupin and golden Poppies, weaving them into my hair. He unbuttons my white gauze dress, and it gently floats down around my feet. As I step out of it, I unbutton his shirt and begin to lovingly kiss his chest. Unbeknownst to him, he is about to fulfill one of my long-time fantasies. With the warm sun beating on our bodies, we lay among the fragrant blossoms tickling one another with the heads of wildflowers and unhurriedly softly kissing. Returning to our canoe, I place the ingredients for our lunch in a glass jar and set it on the bow of the canoe in the sun. As we wait for the sun to "cook" our lunch, we sit in our canoe, me on his lap, picking up where we left off.

Sun-Dried Tomato Oil
- 8 tomatoes chopped
- 3 cloves garlic chopped fine
- 3 shallots chopped
- 1 cup extra virgin olive oil
- 2 tablespoons Balsamic vinegar & red wine vinegar
- ¼ cup fresh basil cut into julienne
- ¼ cup finely chopped Italian leaf parsley
- cracked pepper to taste
- 1 teaspoon salt

Put all of the ingredients in a gallon glass jar. Cover tightly and set in the sun for 6 hours.

Pasta
- 1 lb. fresh fettuccine cooked, rinsed, drained, and kept warm
- ½ lb. chunk Asiago cheese

Place tomato mixture in a pan and heat. Pour over warm linguini and pass the Asiago cheese. *Serves 6*

Linguini with Leeks & Roasted Garlic Oil Surprise

The old adage "necessity is the mother of invention" is surely true in this case. One night as my lover and I lay on our air mattresses in the pool, we realized that we had exhausted our supply of massage oil. Yearning to feel his flesh beneath my hands, I offered him a bottle of my homemade garlic olive oil. We slowly, very slowly rub the oil on the mattress. Then we each slowly spread the oil on our own bodies, watching one another. Frolicking for hours, the scent mixed with the taste of the oil reassured me of concerns to never again be out of massage oil when we were poolside!

- 1 lb. fresh linguini cooked, rinsed, drained, and kept warm
- 1 bunch leeks white part only
- ¼ cup garlic oil
- 1 head roasted garlic smashed
- 1 teaspoon salt
- ¼ cup capers
- ¼ cup extra virgin olive oil
- ¼ cup Chardonnay
- 1 tablespoon fresh oregano leaves

Wash and trim leeks removing outer leaves. Brush with garlic oil and grill over hot coals until soft. Slice into ¼ inch thickness. Place in a bowl with the roasted garlic and stir to combine the ingredients. Add a teaspoon of salt, the capers, extra virgin olive oil, and Chardonnay. Then season with cracked pepper. Place all ingredients in a pan and then heat and toss with pasta. Sprinkle oregano leaves over the top. *Serves 6*

Shallot & Garlic Smashed Red Potatoes

And there we sat at the very top of the bleachers under our comfy, soft lap robe, wildly yelling for our favorite team. The muscles of his legs, under his tight-fitting jeans, would contract and expand with excitement each time our team scored a play. I felt it was time to score a play of my own. Slowly sliding my hand to the inside of his thigh, seductively suggesting his complete attention, I quietly whispered in his ear that it was time for us to play our own game. We hastily left the stadium and found our much-loved location. After indulging in our preferred sport, it was time to replenish our energy with shallots, garlic, and mashed potatoes.

- 2 lbs red potatoes washed and cut into 1½ inch chunks

- 4 shallots peeled and sliced thin
- ½ cup cream
- 2 tablespoons salted butter
- 6 cloves minced peeled garlic
- white pepper and salt to taste

Place potatoes and shallots into a pot of cold water. Bring to a boil and reduce to medium heat. Cook until potatoes are tender. While potatoes are cooking, heat cream, butter, and garlic. Drain the potatoes and shallots and place them in a bowl. Mash with a hand masher. Gradually add the warmed liquid, smashing continuously. Season the potatoes with white pepper and salt. *Serves 4*

Yam & Serrano-Chili Fritters with Creamy Lime Cilantro Sauce

Having fun, we cross-country ski to our forbidden, private hideaway. Carefully he spreads out his thick winter parka and lightly pats it, tempting me to sit beside him. After casually snacking on these fritters, he presses the cold, icy snow into my hot mouth. As it rolls off my lower lip, he bends over, and using his tongue as a snowplow, he pushes his way to the insides of my mouth. As he bears down on my quivering body, I whisper to him, "I'm just warming up!". Just as the right amount of pepper keeps you coming back for more, so do our cross-country trips!

- 4 cups fresh yams cooked and mashed
- ¼ cup honey
- 1 white onion minced and 4 toes minced garlic sautéed in 3 tablespoons olive oil
- 1 cup grated Jack cheese
- 2 cups bread crumbs
- 2 eggs beaten
- cup shucked corn
- cup grated Jack cheese
- minced Serrano chili
- ½ cup minced red bell pepper
- peanut oil for frying fritters

Combine all the ingredients until well mixed. Form the mixture into round cakes using your hands. Heat the peanut oil in a pan, using just enough oil to cover the bottom of the pan. Add more oil as needed. Fry each cake on both sides until golden brown over medium heat. Serve with Peach Chutney. *Makes 12 cakes*

Peach Chutney
- 1 peach peeled and pitted
- ½ small red onion minced
- ½ bunch chopped cilantro
- 2 tablespoons lime juice

Coarsely chop the peach. Add the red onion, cilantro, and lime juice. Mix well. *Makes ¾ cup*

CHAPTER SIX
STEAMY ENCOUNTERS
Vegetables

Emerging from the lake, his body steamy from the warm sun, I catch a glimpse of him as the water drips from his loins. The early morning sun, reflecting the sparkle of the multi-colored rocks, marries the array of voluptuous vegetables that lie in the lofty, parched grass.

Aphrodisiac Chilled Steamed Asparagus with Rice Vinegar Caper Sauce

In the spring, when green asparagus is plentiful, I freely indulge myself several times. As I twirl my tongue around the purple shaft, I want to savor every nibble before I take that first bite.

- 2 lb asparagus, steamed and chilled
- 2 tablespoons diced parsley
- ¼ cup olive oil
- 1 tablespoon capers
- 1 tablespoon rice wine vinegar
- 2 shallots, minced
- 1 tablespoon lemon juice
- 4 toes garlic, minced
- 1 teaspoon Dijon mustard
- salt and fresh cracked pepper to taste

Whisk together the oil, vinegar, and lemon juice. Stir in the remaining ingredients. Lay the asparagus on a platter and pour the sauce on top. Toss to coat each spear. *Serves 4-6*

Sizzling Sesame Asparagus

When thinking our relationship had begun to fizzle, I removed the sash from my long, silk, golden Kimono. As it gracefully slipped off my delicate body, I drew a hot soaking bath for my love and fed him these Asian-tasting spears. We were sizzling once again. Thank you, Karma Sutra.

- 1 lb asparagus
- ¼ cup sesame oil
- 2 tablespoons toasted sesame seeds

Break off the tough ends of the asparagus ends. Wash the spears and pat dry. Brush each spear with the sesame oil and broil for 2 minutes per side. Remove the spears from the broiler and place them on a dish sprinkled with sesame seeds. *Serves 3 to 4*

Blistering Baby Carrots in Orange, Ginger, and Ginseng Sauce

Carrots seem to be more undressed than most root vegetables. My blistering baby loves the sweltering taste of this sexy sauce. The ginseng brings the root to life. Oh, how I love this carrot!

- 1 lb baby carrots
- 2 tablespoons butter
- 1 tablespoon sesame seeds

Wash baby carrots and pat dry. Butter a baking dish with 1 tablespoon butter. Lay the carrots in a pan and dot with the remaining butter. Bake at 375 degrees until tender, about 25 minutes. Remove from the oven. Sprinkle with sesame seeds.

Ginger Ginseng Sauce
- ½ cup orange juice
- 1 teaspoon grated fresh ginger
- 1 teaspoon grated orange rind
- 1 teaspoon sugar
- ½ cup brewed ginseng tea

Add the orange juice, ginseng tea, orange rind, ginger, and sugar to a saucepan. Cook over medium heat. Boil for 1 minute. Add the sesame carrots. Stir to coat and serve. *Serves 6*

Medley of Grilled Baby Zucchini, Patty Pan, and Crookneck Squash

Tempting, tantalizing artistry in its presentation captures the masterpiece of the male anatomy. When my lover offered this to me, I got just what I was searching for!

Vegetable
- 1 lb each baby zucchini, patty pan, and crookneck squashes

Sauce
- ½ cup olive oil
- 3 tablespoons red wine vinegar
- 1 tablespoon balsamic vinegar
- 2 tablespoons diced Italian leaf parsley
- 8 basil leaves, julienne
- 1 tablespoon fresh oregano

Shake the above ingredients in a jar. Place the vegetables in a container and marinate with the sauce for at least 2 hours at room temperature. Place the vegetables in a bar-b-que basket and grill over hot heat until crisp and tender. *Serves 8*

Fresh Cream Corn

I never walk the rolling cornfield alone when gathering baskets of sweet corn. Reaching for the long, stiff cob was always a creamy sensation.

- 4 ears white corn
- 2 tablespoons butter
- 2 cups heavy cream
- salt and pepper to taste

Husk the corn. Remove one end and stand the ear in an upright position on a plate. Using a sharp knife, begin at the top of the cob and slice down the ear to the bottom. Rotate until all of the kernels have been removed. Scrape the cob several times to remove as much starch as possible. Repeat until all the ears have been stripped. Place the corn in a pan. Add the butter and cream and cook over low heat until the corn is thoroughly heated and the mixture thickens eight to ten minutes. Season the corn with salt and pepper.

Explosive French-Fried Onion Star with Ginger Mango Chutney Dipping Sauce

I love to serve this on the Fourth of July. As the darkness of the night takes over, we spread my star-spangled quilt on the ground and get ready for the fireworks. I snuggled next to my soldier and waited for the explosion to go off in my mouth.

- 1 large white onion
- peanut oil for deep frying

Place the onion on a cutting board. Cut through the middle of the onion about ¾ of the way down. Rotate the entire onion. Make the same cut in the opposite direction. Turning the onion in quarter turns, cut through the center again ¾ of the way, making sure to not cut through the entire onion. Place the onion in a jar and cover with water. Chill overnight. Drain the water from the onion. Turn the onion upside down to drain out the excess water. Dip in the batter and deep fry until golden brown.

Batter
- 1 cup flour
- 1 egg
- pinch of salt and pepper
- ¾ cup club soda
- 1 tablespoon vegetable oil

Place the dry ingredients in a bowl. Add the club soda, egg, and oil. Whisk until smooth. Coat the entire onion with the batter. Shake off any excess butter and deep fry.

Mango Chutney Sauce
- ¼ cup white raisins
- 2 tablespoons minced red onion
- ¼ cup orange juice
- 2 mangos peeled and diced
- 1 tablespoon brown sugar
- ¼ teaspoon curry
- 2 tablespoons fig vinegar
- ½ teaspoon cumin

Place all the ingredients in a pan. Stir and cook on medium-low heat for 5 minutes. Remove from pan and serve at room temperature or chill. *Serves 2*

Sporty Anchovy Buttered Green Beans

Sporting only my netted fishing vest and hiking boots, I grab his pole, and off we go! Who said anchovies are only for Caesar and his salad?

- 1 lb string beans, washed and trimmed
- ¼ cup lemon juice
- water
- 1 tablespoon grated lemon rind
- ¼ cup butter
- 2 teaspoons fresh, cracked pepper
- 3 cloves chopped garlic
- salt to taste
- 1 tablespoon anchovy paste
- ½ cup grated Asiago cheese

Cook the beans until crisp and tender in a large pot of boiling water. Drain and keep warm. Melt the butter in a pan over medium-low heat. Add the garlic, anchovy paste, lemon rind, and juice, and stir. Add the beans. Season with cracked pepper and salt. Place in a bowl and sprinkle the cheese on top. *Serves 4*

Turn-Me-On Chilled Artichokes with Lemon Aioli

Turning the hot tub on to get the bubbles churning and pouring two chilled glasses of Chardonnay, I call my sweetheart to join me. As we experienced the sensation of pulling the chilled leaves lightly through our lower teeth and pursed lips, we began to really get excited. A little smear with the aioli always works for us.

- 2 artichokes
- 1 peeled garlic
- water
- 1 teaspoon olive oil
- 2 slices of lemon

Cut the stem from the bottom of the artichoke. Lay the artichoke flat on its side and cut away the top inch. Then use a pair of scissors to snip the points off the remaining leaves. Place the artichokes in a pot, and cover with water. Add the garlic, lemon, and oil. Cook over medium heat until tender, about 30-45 minutes. Remove from the water, and turn it upside down to drain. Chill

Lemon Aioli
- 2 eggs
- ½ cup lemon juice
- zest of 1 lemon
- 2 cups olive oil
- salt and pepper to taste

Place the eggs and lemon juice in a processor. Turn the process on and add the oil through the fed tube. Once the oil has been incorporated into the mixture, place the aioli in a bowl and fold in the lemon zest. Season the aioli with salt and pepper.

Ohhhhh…. Eggplant with Pine Nuts, Tomatoes, Olives, & Onions

Oh, what a dish! As I prepare this curvaceous globed vegetable, he quietly approaches from behind, and passionately, he embraces my voluptuous bulbs. I love having a man in the kitchen.

- 2 medium eggplants
- 18 chopped stuffed green olives
- 4 ribs thinly sliced celery
- 2 coarsely chopped large tomatoes
- 3 medium white onions chopped
- 1/3 cup red wine vinegar
- ¼ cup olive oil
- 1 tablespoon pine nuts
- 4 minced garlic toes
- 3 tablespoons caper
- 18 Kalamata olives, chopped
- 1 teaspoon salt and pepper

Cut the eggplants into ½-inch cubes and set them aside. Place the celery and onions in a pan and sauté in two tablespoons of hot olive oil. When vegetables are soft, add the garlic and continue to sauté. Remove the vegetables and place them in a small pan. Place the eggplant into the same pan and sauté in the remaining olive oil. Add the olives, sautéed vegetables, and tomatoes. Add the vinegar, pine nuts, capers, and salt and pepper. Simmer until most of the liquid has been absorbed and the eggplant is tender. *Serves 4 to 6*

Lusty Lemon Spinach Sauté'

Grating the rind over the finished food alerted my beloved to gently drag his manicured nails down my bronze bareback. This sensation caused chills to run up and down my wavering body. As his luscious lips softly kissed the nape of my neck, I, too, wilted from the heat, much like the spinach.

- 1 tablespoon butter mixed with 1 tablespoon lemon zest
- ¼ cup diced white onions
- 1 teaspoon salt and lemon pepper
- 2 bunches spinach
- juice of 1 lemon

Melt butter in a pan. Sauté the onion until soft, and add the salt and pepper. Wash, de-stem, and dry the spinach. Add to the sautéed onion. Pour on the lemon juice and cook until the spinach wilts. *Serves 2*

Satisfy Me Broccoli & Grilled Portabella Mushrooms in Cabernet Cream Pepper Sauce

Picking wild mushrooms with my honey has always been a juicy experience. I always made sure to carry a guidebook for recognizing the edible ones. Of course, I didn't need this when searching under his cap. I always recognized it as being delectably edible!

Vegetables
- 1 head broccoli
- 1 Portabella mushroom

Remove the broccoli flowers from the stem. Place in a pot of boiling water. As soon as the broccoli turns a rich green color, drain and place in a sink full of ice water. Drain again and set aside. Cut the portabella mushroom into ¼ inch slices. Grill the mushrooms and the broccoli over medium-high heat and baste with the following sauce:

Basting Sauce
- 2 tablespoons melted butter
- 1 tablespoon Dijon mustard
- 1 tablespoon chopped chervil

Peppercorn Cream Sauce
- 2 tablespoons butter
- 2 tablespoons Merlot wine
- 2 minced garlic toes
- 1 cup cream

- 2 tablespoons minced red onion
- ½ cup Gorgonzola cheese
- 1 tablespoon cracked pepper

Melt the butter in a pan. Add the garlic and onion and sauté until soft. Add the pepper and Merlot and cook until most of the Merlot is absorbed. Add the cream and stir until it is well heated for five to seven minutes. Lay the broccoli and portabella mushrooms in a nonglass baking pan. Pour the cream sauce over the top. Season the sauce with salt to taste and sprinkle with the cheese. Broil until bubbly. *Serves 4*

CHAPTER SEVEN
HOT AND HEAVIES
Entrees

With candlelight flickering to the strumming of his guitar, I lovingly set the hearth for an intimate supper.

Italian Stallion Stuffed Flank

As I sat in a famous Italian restaurant in New York City nonchalantly sipping a glass of Chianti, our eyes locked. I felt the heat of my flushed face as he strutted towards me. His gaze undressing me, I lowered my eyelashes. Much to my surprise, I became the voyeur. To this day, I know that what he had stuffed into his pants was real. That memory inspired this hot creation!

Steak
- 2 lb. flank steak cut with a pocket for stuffing

Marinate
- ½ cup red wine
- 2 tablespoons Dijon mustard
- ¼ cup olive oil
- 4 cloves garlic minced
- 1 bunch fresh oregano

Combine the wine and olive oil with mustard and garlic. Strip the leaves from four stems of oregano and add this to the marinade. Cover steak with the marinade and refrigerate overnight.

Remove the meat from the marinade and shake off the excess liquid. Place it on a cutting board and open the pocket. Stuff the steak with the vegetable stuffing. Roll the stuffed steak into a cylinder and tie it with twine, about every 2 inches. Bake at 350 degrees, forty-five minutes to one hour. Remove the twine from the meat and slice the steak into pinwheels. *Serves 4*

Vegetable Stuffing
- 4 finely chopped shallots
- 1 bunch chopped spinach
- ½ finely diced yellow bell pepper
- 1 beaten egg
- 3 cloves minced garlic
- ¼ cup seasoned breadcrumbs
- ¼ lb thinly sliced mushrooms
- ¼ cup grated Asiago cheese
- 2 tablespoons sun-dried tomato oil & tomatoes
- 1 teaspoon salt
- 4 stems fresh oregano
- ¼ teaspoon cracked black pepper

Sauté the shallots, pepper, garlic, and mushrooms in the oil. When soft, add the spinach, which has been washed and spun dry. Remove the leaves from the stems of the oregano and add them to the mixture. Season the stuffing with salt and pepper. When the spinach has wilted, remove it from the heat, and mix in the sun-dried tomatoes. Place the mixture in a bowl and let it cool. Add the egg, breadcrumbs, and grated cheese. Combine thoroughly.

More Than Tender Beef Tenderloin with Horseradish Sauce

My tender guy loves meat and potatoes. After scoring with his tender loins, we horse around a little bit more, creating a creamy sauce. This meal always scores in my direction.

Beef Tenderloin
- 2 lb whole beef tenderloin
- 1 bunch chives
- ¼ cup Dijon mustard
- 1 teaspoon salt
- ¼ cup capers
- 4 slices peppered bacon
- 2 tablespoons mixed peppercorns coarsely ground

Place beef on a cutting board. Using a sharp knife, make a lengthwise cut through the middle from the top of the tenderloin to the bottom of the tenderloin, being sure to not cut all the way through. The fillet is now butterflied. Open the beef and press the beef flat, exposing the inside. Spread the Dijon mustard on the inside of the beef. Lay the chives on one side of the beef. Sprinkle with peppercorns, capers, and salt. Lay two strips of bacon over the chives. Fold the top half of the beef over the bottom half of the beef. Lay the remaining bacon on top of the beef. Tie with twine about every two inches. Roast the beef at 375 degrees for 45 minutes to 1 hour. Remove from the oven. Cut away the twine and slice the beef crosswise. Serve with the Horseradish Sauce. *Serves 4*

Horseradish Sauce
- ½ pint fresh cream
- 2 to 4 tablespoons prepared horseradish

Place the cream into a chilled mixing bowl. Whip on high speed until peaks form. Fold in the horseradish. *Makes 1½ cups*

Pleasing Pork for a Pleasing Evening

Once I remember being in a sweltering jam with my sweet "Sumo." I staged an oriental evening amidst the bamboo garden with flowing silk scarves, burning sandalwood incense, an oriental pleasure book for lovers, cherry-flavored body butter, and of course, this pleasing pork. He contentedly said, "Ah-So" many times over.

Pork
- 2 lb boneless pork tenderloin
- 1 fresh pineapple

Marinade
- 2 tablespoons soy sauce
- 4 cloves minced garlic
- ¼ cup sherry
- 1 tablespoon grated fresh ginger
- 1 teaspoon Chinese mustard
- 2 tablespoons sesame oil
- 1 tablespoon sesame seeds
- ¼ cup apricot jam

Place the marinated ingredients in a saucepan and cook on medium heat, occasionally stirring, until thoroughly heated. Cool completely. Place pork in a zip lock bag and pour the marinade over the pork. Place in the refrigerator and marinate overnight. Lay the pork in a shallow baking pan and bake in a preheated oven at 350 degrees for 45 minutes. Baste the pork every fifteen minutes with the remaining marinate. Slice the pork and serve with fresh pineapple slices. *Serves 4*

Herb Crusted Naked Rib Eye

Removing the sweaty red bandanna from my cowboy's neck and tying his wrists, I seized the opportunity to ride his bucking bronco, my eyes feasted on his naked ribs. My, how delicious a nudist dude ranch can be!

Steak
- 4 clove minced garlic
- 1 teaspoon crushed green peppercorn
- ½ teaspoon salt
- 1 tablespoon Dijon mustard
- 1 bunch rosemary
- 2 tablespoons chopped parsley
- 1 bunch oregano
- ½ cup olive oil
- 2 one-pound boneless rib-eye steaks

Mash the garlic and salt to form a paste. Add two teaspoons of rosemary and oregano, and then add the green peppercorns. Mix well. Add the Dijon mustard, parsley, and olive oil. Mix until thick paste forms. Place the steak in a flat container and spread the paste evenly on both sides. Cover and refrigerate overnight. Grill or broil the steaks to the desired doneness. Rare-5 minutes per side Medium – 8 minutes per side
Well done – 10 minutes per side. *Serves 2*
Serve with Glaze Kelle.

Glaze Kelle
- 2 lbs cracked beef bones
- 1 bunch marjoram
- bottle red wine
- 1 bunch parsley
- 1 unpeeled medium red onion
- 1 bunch thyme
- 8 cloves smashed garlic
- 8 whole black peppercorns
- 2 teaspoons salt

Place all the ingredients except the wine in a large pot. Add water to cover and simmer for 8 to 9 hours. Strain the liquid. When cool, place in the refrigerator and chill overnight. Remove the fat from the top of the liquid. Measure and mix the remaining liquid with equal parts of red wine. Cook over medium heat until the mixture is reduced by half. *Makes 2 cups*

Apple of My Eye Pork Spareribs

Standing on the top rung of the red wooden ladder with outstretched arms, I grabbed the last golden apple as it dangled from the bare branch. Standing below me, eagerly stroking the insides of my sheer white nylon-covered thighs, he pulls on the long strand of shiny pearls draped around my bare neck. Gingerly he guides me down the ladder and carries me under the tree.

Instantaneously our bodies are entwined. From that day forward, I was the apple of his eye!

Spareribs
- 2 lbs country-style pork spareribs

Dried Marinade
- 2 teaspoons garlic powder
- ½ teaspoon cardamom
- 1 teaspoon salt
- ½ teaspoon dried thyme
- ¼ teaspoon ground white pepper
- ½ teaspoon ground nutmeg
- ¼ teaspoon ground cloves
- ½ teaspoon cinnamon

Combine all the ingredients in a bowl. Rub the marinade on both sides of the ribs. Place the ribs in the refrigerator and let them set for two hours. While the ribs are setting, make the glaze.

Glaze
- 1 thinly sliced white onion
- 1/3cup apple cider
- ½ cup apple cider vinegar
- 1 tablespoon brown sugar
- 1 grated apple
- 2 tablespoons Calvados
- 2 tablespoons honey

Place the onion, vinegar, apple cider, apple, honey, and brown sugar in a saucepan. Bring to a boil over medium heat. Reduce heat to low and cook uncovered, occasionally stirring until the mixture is reduced to a half cup. Add the Calvados. Place the ribs in a baking pan. Brush with the glaze. Bake the ribs at 350 degrees for 15 minutes. Turn the ribs and brush the other side with the glaze. Bake the ribs for 15 minutes. Repeat this process until the ribs have baked for a total of one hour. Serve with any remaining glaze. *Serves 4*

Pork Loin with Headless Beer Sauce

Our visit to the local microbrewery was a heady experience. After going on the tour, we decided to quench our thirst. I studied the brew master as he tilted the Pilsner glass and expertly poured the brew. Now contemplating the foamy head on the beer, I couldn't wait to have my own heady experience!

Pork Loin
- 3 lb pork loin

Marinade
- 1 large chopped white onion
- 3 cups flat beer
- 4 garlic cloves
- 1/2 cup honey
- ½ teaspoon dry mustard
- leaves stripped from one bunch pineapple thyme

Place all of the above ingredients in a pan and bring to a boil stirring occasionally. Remove the mixture from the heat and let it cool. When cooled, puree the marinade in a blender. Place the pork in a bowl. Pour the marinade over the pork and refrigerate overnight. Turn once the next morning. Preheat the oven to 425 degrees. Remove the pork loin from the marinade and pat it dry.

Coating
Combine:
- 1 teaspoon salt
- ½ teaspoon ground pepper
- 1 tablespoon dried thyme

Add this to:
- 2 tablespoons soften butter.
- 2 tablespoons flour

Sprinkle the flour on the butter mixture and combine well.

Rub this on the outside of the roast and place it on a rack in a roasting pan. Bake for fifteen minutes. Reduce heat to 375 degrees and continue cooking for one hour, basting with the remaining marinate every fifteen minutes. Remove the roast from the oven and place it on a platter.

Deglaze the roasting pan

Pour ¼ cup of warm beer into the roasting pan scraping up the brown bits from the bottom of the pan. Add the remaining marinade and cook until the mixture is reduced to ½ cup.

Surround the roast with caramelized onions, dried cranberries, and sautéed wild mushrooms. Pour the sauce over the sliced meat.

Chicken Breasts in Lemon Caper Sauce

Yellow is one of his favorite colors so having a day of yellow occurrences was another way to please him. I set a small table at the edge of our lawn and adorned it with a crisp yellow linen cloth. Placing a bouquet of yellow tulips in the center, after setting the table with yellow Fiesta Ware, I made a path of baby yellow daisy heads for him to follow from his hammock to the lawn. A tiara of yellow roses adorned my dark brown hair, and

lemon oil anointed my olive skin. What else could I have served him but Lemon Chicken?

- 2 whole skinless, boneless breasts
- 1 cube butter
- ¼ cup flour
- juice and zest of 4 lemons
- teaspoon cracked green peppercorns
- ½ cup Chardonnay
- 2 tablespoons garlic powder
- ½ cup capers, drained
- 1 teaspoon salt
- ½ cup chopped parsley

Wash chicken breasts and pat dry. Place flour, garlic, salt, and pepper in a small lunch-size bag. Shake to combine thoroughly. Place the chicken in a bag one piece at a time and shake to thoroughly coat. Melt the butter in a pan over medium heat. Add the chicken pieces and cook to a golden brown on both sides. Remove the chicken from the pan and set it aside. Add lemon juice, zest, wine, capers, and parsley to the pan and cook, scraping up the brown bits from the pan. Continue to cook until the sauce is thick. Divide the sauce evenly over the chicken breast and serve. *Serves 4*

Rosy Almond Chicken Breasts with Hollandaise Sauce

Our first anniversary was a most memorable affair. To set the stage, I carried throw pillows to the rose garden. After placing them on an antique burgundy-colored spread, I draped the mattress with luxurious virgin, white, satin sheets sprinkled with fresh pink and scarlet rose petals. With the music of the pond spilling and splashing over the rocks, I arranged aromatic candles among the rosebushes and onto the lawn around the bed. Dipping the breasts in the succulent sauce, he savored every delicious morsel. His tongue traces the contours of the breast with complete and utter contentment. Later, after counting the shooting stars from our romantic garden bedroom, we enjoy dinner from a silver tray, our meal as elegant as our surroundings.

Chicken
- 2 boneless, skinless chicken breasts cut in half
- ¼ teaspoon white pepper
- 2 teaspoons garlic powder
- 1 teaspoon salt
- 4 tablespoons flour

Wash the chicken breast and pat them dry. Season the chicken with garlic, salt, and pepper and lightly coat them with flour. Set aside.

Batter
- 4 eggs
- ¾ cup flour
- 1 teaspoon paprika

Beat the eggs with the paprika. Add the flour, ¼ cup at a time, until thoroughly combined. Dip the chicken breasts into the batter, shaking off any excess. Roll each breast in the following combination

Coating
- 1½ pounds finely minced slivered almonds
- 4 tablespoons of rose water

Mix the almonds with rose water.
- 1 stick butter
- ¼ cup extra virgin olive oil

Melt the butter and olive oil over low heat. After the chicken is coated, cook the breasts until golden brown on each side. Remove from the pan and place on a serving platter. Pour the Hollandaise sauce over the chicken and sprinkle with edible rose petals.

Hollandaise Sauce
- 3 egg yolks
- ¼ cup chardonnay
- ½ cup butter
- 2 tablespoons fresh lemon juice
- salt and pepper to taste

Heat the wine and lemon juice. Melt the butter and keep warm. Beat the egg yolks and place them in the top half of a double boiler. Beat the yolks again until they are thick and lemon colored. Add the liquid one tablespoon at a time mixing well with a wire whisk.

Slowly add the butter, beating continually. Season the sauce with salt and pepper. Continue to beat until the mixture is thick.

Serve at once. If it must be stored using a thermos to keep the sauce warm.

Quiet Affair Broiled Game Hens with Pomegranate Sauce

Our first Christmas Eve together was a very private and quiet affair, unlike many that I had spent in past years. It was so unusual for me not to have the hustle and bustle that this time of the year brings. By the end of the evening, I was enchanted that it had only been the two of us. He had given me the best gift

of all, the gift of himself, which inspired me to create an unforgettable Christmas Eve offering for him.

Game Hens
- 2 Cornish game hens washed, patted dry, and butter flied
- 4 tablespoons butter melted
- 3 minced cloves garlic
- ½ teaspoon powdered ginger
- 1 teaspoon salt

Melt the butter. Add the salt, garlic, and ginger and stir to prevent burning. Broil the game hens basting with the butter mixture until they are golden brown, about 15 minutes per side.

Pomegranate Sauce
- 1 cup chicken stock
- juice of half a lime
- ¼ cup honey
- zest of 1 lime
- ¼ cup pomegranate juice
- Seeds from one half of a pomegranate, white part discarded

Place the above ingredients into a sauce pan and cook until thick. Place the game hens on a platter and pour the sauce on the top. Garnish with the seeds of the other half of the pomegranate and wedges of lime.

Mediterranean Chicken with Sun-Dried Tomato Pesto

Although his culinary skills are underdeveloped, cooking together is always entertaining. Because of his love for tomatoes, this was a food he thoroughly enjoys. Wearing only our scant red aprons, we have a most enjoyable time pinching and squeezing the merchandise!

Chicken
- 3 - 4 lb whole chicken
- 1 tablespoon dried rosemary
- 1 tablespoon dried basil
- 2 teaspoons salt
- 1 tablespoon dried oregano
- 1 teaspoon cracked black pepper
- 1 tablespoon dried parsley
- ½ cup olive oil
- 1 tablespoon dried marjoram
- 2 lemons cut in half
- 1 bunch parsley washed and dried

Wash the inside and outside of the chicken and pat it dry. Pour a couple of tablespoons of olive oil into the cavity of the chicken. Combine the dry herbs with salt and pepper. Sprinkle half of the mixture inside the chicken. Place the bunch of parsley into the cavity of the chicken. Squeeze the juice of the lemons into the cavity and place the lemons inside of the cavity also. Rub the outside of the chicken with the remaining olive oil. Sprinkle the dried herb mixture over the chicken. Roast on a rack in a preheated oven at 375 degrees for 60-75 minutes.

Sun Dried Tomato Pesto
- 5 diced tomatoes
- 3 tablespoons extra virgin olive oil
- 5 cloves minced garlic
- 1 tablespoon sun-dried tomato oil
- ¼ cup chopped basil and flat leaf parsley
- 5 chopped sun-dried tomatoes that have been removed from their olive oil

Combine the above ingredients and stir to blend

Assembling

Remove the chicken from the oven and cut it into quarters. Spoon the sun-dried tomato pesto over each quarter. Garnish with a fresh basil leaf. *Serves 4*

Kibbee (Ground Lamb) with a Yogurt Mint Sauce

Serving this lamb dish with the exotic sounds of Arabic music and anise-flavored liqueur on the Persian carpet in our tent put me in a tribal state of mind. I titillated him with the sensual undulating movement of my belly dancing. Dancing by the light of the bonfire aroused peals of laughter, causing us to fall teasingly to the ground, holding each other and rolling in the sand, which stimulated our passion.

Kibbee
- 3 lbs of ground lamb
- 1 cup fine grain cracked wheat
- 1 large white onion
- 1 tablespoon allspice

- 4 cloves of garlic
- 2 teaspoons salt
- ½ teaspoon round pepper
- 1 cup pine nuts
- 2 tablespoons melted butter

Melt the butter in a pan. Add the pine nuts and heat until warm. Remove from the heat and let cool. Place the ground lamb in a bowl. Add the seasonings and combine. Cover the cracked wheat with water. Let this sit until the cracked wheat is soft, about 10-15 minutes. Place the onion in a processor and chop until almost pulverized. Add the lamb to the processor and pulse three or four times until the lamb and onions are well combined. Return to the bowl. Drain the cracked wheat and squeeze out any excess water using your hands. Add this to the lamb mixture. Mix well. Divide the lamb mixture in half. Spread half of the lamb into a 9 x 13-inch pan. Sprinkle the pine nuts on top. Cover with the remaining lamb spreading it out to make a rectangular shape. Cut a line through the center of the lamb lengthwise and crosswise. Beginning at the center, cut a diagonal line to the bottom corner. Do this to the remaining three sections. Cut each quarter section into diagonal strips about one inch apart, beginning at the center. Bake at 350 degrees for 1 hour.

Yogurt Mint Sauce
- large clove of garlic
- cup plain yogurt
- ½ teaspoon salt
- 2 tablespoons dried mint

Smash the garlic clove in a medium size bowl. Sprinkle with salt. Smash the garlic clove and the salt together several times. Add the yogurt and mix again. Sprinkle with the dried mint. Serve with the lamb. *Serves 10*

Le Fleur Lamb with Lemon Sauce

I served this the first night that spring invited us to eat outdoors. Mixing stems of fresh cut mint among the le fleur, I place the bouquet in the breast pocket of his white terry bathrobe. This is a zesty entrée with just the right amount of lemon flavor.

Lamb
- 1 5lb leg of lamb boned and butter flied
- ¼ cup crumbled dried mint
- juice and zest of five lemons
- 6 cloves smashed garlic
- leaves removed from 2 springs fresh rosemary

Combine all the ingredients except the lamb. Place the lamb in a rectangular pan and pour marinade on top. Place in the refrigerator. Turn after four hours. Marinate for another four hours. Place the lamb and marinate into an oven-roasting bag and bake at 350 degrees for one hour. Remove lamb from the bag and slice thin. Serve with Lemon Sauce.

Lemon Sauce
- 1 teaspoon cumin seed
- 2 cloves chopped garlic
- juice of 1 lemon
- 2 tablespoons extra virgin olive oil
- 3 tablespoons julienne fresh mint
- 6 chopped Kalamata olives
- 6 chopped pimento-stuffed olives

Combine all ingredients. Let this sit for about one hour. Stir and serve on top of the lamb slices. Garnish with edible flowers.

Blanco Prawns

My dear friend owns a fleet of shrimp boats off the Keys of Florida. Watching the laden nets being pulled up from the foamy sea with this mouth-watering delicacy made me truly appreciate how distinguished a recipe must be to honor this ultimate sacrifice. The best thing about shelling the shrimp was showering with my fabulous fisherman as the sun set over the shore.

Prawns
- 2 tablespoons melted butter
- ½ cup Fume wine
- 12 prawns (under 15 to a pound, extra-large size)
- 2 tablespoons of Pernod
- 6 peeled and sliced pearl onions
- 1 cup cream

- ½ teaspoon salt
- ¼ teaspoon ground white pepper
- 2 teaspoons vanilla sugar

    Devine and butterfly the prawns. Wash and pat dry. Melt the butter in a pan. Sauté the prawns just until they turn pink. Remove from the pan. Add the onions to the pan and sauté until soft. Add the wine, Pernod, sugar, cream, salt, and pepper and cook, reducing to one-half. Return the prawns to the pan and stir to coat with the sauce. *Serves 4*

Stormy Scallop Scampi

Cuddling on the beach after a passing gale, the flickering light of a roaring bonfire surrounds us, and we inhale the distinctive smell that only the ocean can offer. After a pleasurable meal, adorned with only my clamshell necklace, as he requested, I shyly sit closer to my salty sea captain. We gaze across the horizon and share stories of sailing ventures we had yet to take. He excitedly pulls my necklace from around my neck, and then he gifts me with a pearl necklace as a token of an adventure just unfolded. Clamshells are a wonderful serving vessel for this dish

Scampi
- 1 lb scallops, washed and patted dry
- 2 tablespoons parsley
- 1 cube butter
- juice of 3 fresh lemons
- 1 onion peeled, washed, and finely chopped
- 2 sprigs fresh baby dill
- 4 cloves minced garlic
- salt and white pepper to taste
- 2 ribs celery, washed and finely chopped

Melt one-half of the cube of butter in a pan. Add the onions, celery, and garlic. Sauté until the vegetables are soft. Melt the rest of the butter in the same pan and add the scallops. Continue to cook until the scallops have lost their opaque appearance, 3 to 5 minutes. Add the lemon juice and parsley. Season the scampi and divide it into two clamshells. Garnish with springs of baby dill that have been placed in the center of lemon rounds. *Serves 2*

Tsunami* Salmon with Pineapple Cilantro Salsa

A lei of intoxicating scented white yellow plumeria foliage dangling from my neck and a square of colorful Hawaiian print fabric wrapped around my robust hips set the scene for our Luau for Two. We make beverage containers from freshly cut sweet pineapples and display a platter of perfectly ripe star fruit, papaya, and mangos. He quietly strums on his ukulele while humming his favorite Hawaiian love song. I serve this delectable salmon as our main course. Placing a garland of lush Ti leaves and beads on my beloved's head, I invite him to dance. Hula dancing will cause a* Tsunami you can't control!

   * Hawaiian for storm

Salmon
- 4-pound salmon skinned and filleted

Wash the salmon and pat it dry. Line a cookie sheet with parchment paper. Place the salmon on top of the paper. Baste with glaze. Bake at 350 degrees for 20 to 25 minutes, basting every five minutes. *Serves 6*

Glaze
- ¼ cup sesame oil
- 2 tablespoons sesame seeds
- ½ cup of honey
- ¼ cup of soy sauce

Place all of the ingredients in a bowl and combine thoroughly.

Pineapple Cilantro Salsa
- ¼ finely chopped fresh pineapple
- ¼ finely chopped honeydew
- ¼ finely minced red bell pepper
- Kernels from one half ear white corn
- ¼ cup coarsely chopped cilantro
- juice of 1 lime

Place the pineapple and honeydew in a bowl and add the pepper, corn, cilantro, and lime juice. Stir to combine. Arrange the salsa next to the salmon. *Makes one cup.*

Raging Roast of Halibut with Blackberry Lime Sauce

Taking the ferry across the Seattle Harbor to encounter my darling was as exciting for me as it was gratifying for him. Dressed only in a soft fur overcoat, I was extremely nervous upon arriving at my destination. There he stood with a bundle of newspaper-wrapped fish under one arm and a basket of berries in his hand. Once we were in the car, I opened my coat, and much to his surprise, I exposed my bare skin. Taking a berry from his basket, he ever so carefully pressed it against my lips. Placing his mouth on mine caused the juice from the berry to trickle down my chin and under my throat. He followed the trail of nectar with his tongue. Every time I cook this dish, I relive that raging passion over and over again.

Halibut
- 3 lb Halibut roast skinned

Glaze
- teaspoon five spice
- ½ teaspoon anise seed
- ½ teaspoon red pepper flakes
- 3 tablespoons fresh lime juice
- 3 tablespoons blackberry syrup
- 2 tablespoons fish sauce
- 1 tablespoon walnut oil

Combine the above ingredients. Place the halibut roast on a bar-b-que grill over indirect heat and grill for 45 minutes. Baste

with the glaze every 10 minutes. Serve with Blackberry Lime Sauce.

Blackberry Lime Sauce
- 1 tablespoon dark brown sugar
- 1/3 cup blackberry jam
- 2 tablespoons sour cream
- zest of 1 lime
- juice of 1 lime
- basket fresh blackberries
- 1 tablespoon chopped walnut

Mix the brown sugar and jam with the sour cream until thoroughly combined. Add the lime juice and the zest. Fold in the blackberries. Top with chopped walnuts.

CHAPTER EIGHT
THE MORNING AFTER
Breakfast

Breakfast with my lover, draped by morning sunlight, brings our "Food Affair" full circle. His warm body pressed against the cool satin sheets invites me to please him once again!

Most Delicious Grand Mariner French Toast with Fig Syrup

As I return this special treatment, lathering his lean body with orange oil, I zest the peel onto his chest. Using my tongue, I spread the zest around his entire torso. Working my way down his body, I dip his toes in Grand Mariner. After sensuously sucking the liquor from his feet, I invite him to breakfast.

Grand Mariner French toast
- ¼ cup Grand Mariner
- 8 tablespoons butter
- zest of 1 orange
- 8 eggs
- ¼ cup sugar
- 1 ¼ cup fresh orange juice and a half and half
- 1 loaf stale sourdough bread, both ends removed, cut into 1-inch slices

In a large shallow bowl, beat the eggs until they are pale yellow. Add the sugar and beat again until the sugar is thoroughly combined. Add the half and half orange juice and Grand Mariner. Mix well. Add the orange zest and stir again. Lay the bread in the liquid and let set for 15 minutes. Turn the bread over and cover. Place in the refrigerator overnight. Melt a couple of tablespoons of butter in a pan until the butter begins to foam. Add the bread and brown it on each side. Repeat with the butter and bread until all the French toast is cooked. *Serves 8*

Tempting Apple Pancakes with Beer Syrup

Rinsing the apple-scented shampoo from my thick, dark hair, we indulge in one of our Sunday morning rituals… our shower. Caressing my earlobe, he whispers to me to close my eyes. As he kisses the beads of water from my eyelids, he pours warm beer over my head and massages it into my scalp. As I return to this special treatment, I feel a sense of erotica sweep over me. With the water droplets glistening on my apple-smelling skin, I look at him with alluring eyes. He steps out of the shower and lays a bath sheet on the wooden bathroom floor. He then motions for me to lie down. Since we have worked up an extra ordinary appetite and our nostrils are filled with the scents of apples and beer, it only seems fitting that I prepare this extra ordinary breakfast.

Pancakes
- 4 eggs
- 1 tablespoon brown sugar
- 1 ¾ cup all-purpose flour
- ½ cup buttermilk
- ½ cup beer
- ¼ cup vegetable oil
- 2 grated apples
- zest of 1 lemon

Beat the eggs and sugar until frothy. Combine the milk and beer. Combine the brown sugar and the flour. Alternate the flour and the milk mixture with the eggs. Stir in the oil and mix until well combined. Fold in the apples and lemon zest. Heat a griddle over medium-high heat and coat with oil. Drop ¼ cup of pancake batter onto the grill. When the top bubbles turn and cook the other side to a golden brown. *Serves 4*

Syrup
- ½ cup beer
- 3/4 cup brown sugar
- 3 tablespoons butter
- ½ teaspoon cinnamon

Boil the beer, brown sugar, butter, and cinnamon, stirring frequently. Cool to warm and serve over apple pancakes.

NOTE: For best results, use stale beer. Open the beer the night before you plan to make the syrup and leave it out at room temperature.

Captivating Baked Peach Pancakes with Cranberry Peach Syrup

I love to watch him sleep. His dark tresses lying across the cranberry-colored pillowcase emphasize his peach-colored skin. The soft prickles of his 5 o'clock shadow tease my mouth as I awaken him with a morning kiss. His puffy lips invite me for another. How do I express to him how much I care? By serving

him this breakfast-in-bed creation, made especially with that visual of him in mind.

Pancakes
- 2 eggs
- 1/2 teaspoon grated lemon zest
- 3 tablespoons melted butter
- 3/4 cup sliced peaches
- 1 teaspoon vanilla
- 1 tablespoon orange juice
- 1 tablespoon flour
- 1 tablespoon powdered sugar

Combine the eggs, melted butter, and vanilla. Sprinkle the flour over the top and mix until well combined. Add the lemon zest. Pour into a good butter 8-inch baking pan. Bake in a preheated 375degree oven for 8 to 10 minutes. The pancake will puff up and look cakey. Remove from the oven and invert the pancake onto a plate. Place the sliced peaches over the top and sprinkle with the orange juice. Fold the pancake in half and dust with a tablespoon of powdered sugar. *Makes 1*

Syrup
- 1½ cups fresh cranberries
- ½ cup apricot preserves
- 1 peach seeded and chopped
- ½ cup orange juice

Combine these ingredients in a saucepan and boil gently for 10 minutes. Keep warm and pour over pancakes. *Makes 1 ½ to 2 cups*

Sun Shine California Crab Casserole with Sour Cream Buns

Sitting on the sandy shore, we watched the sun rise over the Atlantic Ocean. As the sea turned from a midnight blue to a golden bronze, we were overcome by its' beauty. Holding one another closely, he slipped his tongue into my mouth, gently searching for an approving response. As we strolled along the water's edge, the cool fluid wrapped itself around our ankles. We listened to the sea lions bark a "good morning" to us. The aroma of the sea encircled us like a cocoon. After that long walk on the beach, we were ready to partake in a meal that only our California customs could express. Dumping the net full of crabs in the kitchen sink, we made preparations for our breakfast. Picking up the claw of the biggest crab, he began to lovingly pinch me. The steam coming from under the lid of the crab pot resembled the way I was feeling on the inside. The peaceful atmosphere of the sea had now turned into a wild raging storm. Our passion had now taken over our hunger. Each time we make this meal, we keep the memory of our east coast sunrise alive!

- 8 slices day old sourdough bread
- 1 cube butter
- ½ lb crab meat
- 2 cups grated Jarlsberg cheese
- 3 beaten eggs
- 2 ½ cups half and half
- 1 teaspoon Dijon mustard
- 1 teaspoon salt
- ½ teaspoon cracked pepper

Set the bread out on a plate uncovered overnight. The next day butter on both sides of the hard bread. Butter a 9-inch square pan. Beat the eggs, half and half, mustard, salt, and pepper. Layer the bread, egg mixture, crab, and cheese, ending with the cheese layer. Repeat. Cover and refrigerate overnight. Bake uncovered at 325 degrees, for 1 hour or until the eggs are set. *Serves 4*

Sour Cream Buns
- ¾ cup sour cream
- 1 package yeast
- 2 tablespoons sugar
- 2 ¼ cups all-purpose flour
- 2 tablespoons butter
- beaten egg
- 1 tablespoon chopped fresh chives
- ¼ cup warm water

Mix the sour cream, sugar, chives, butter, and water in a pan. Heat until boiling, stirring frequently. Remove from the heat and cool until lukewarm. In a large bowl, place the sour cream mixture and half of the flour and the yeast. Beat until smooth. Mix in the remaining flour and egg. Cover and let rise until double in a warm place for about 1 hour. Stir the batter 4 to 5 strokes and spoon unto 12 greased muffin cups filling until half full. Let rise until the batter reaches the top of the cups, approximately 30 minutes. Bake in a preheated oven at 400 degrees for 15 minutes. *Makes 12 rolls*

Ravenous Canadian Bacon Baked Eggs

There he stood, my handsome Mounty dressed in full regalia. Removing his hat, I tenderly kissed both ears. Unbuttoning his jacket ever so slowly, I felt him place his hands on my steady shoulders. As his jacket fell to the floor, my hand undid his belt buckle. The sound of his zipper being released filled my body with anticipation. Mounting his horse, we furiously rode our journey

out. Indulging in this hardy breakfast was very much appreciated after our long, hard ride.

- 4 slices chopped Canadian bacon
- 2 tablespoons butter
- 8 eggs
- ½ cup cream
- ¼ cup Gruyere cheese, grated
- salt and pepper to taste

Butter 4 ramekin dishes. Divide the Canadian bacon evenly among them. Crack 2 eggs in each dish over the ham. Season the eggs with salt and pepper. Place 2 tablespoons of cream over the eggs. Sprinkle each egg dish with 1 tablespoon of cheese. Bake in a preheated oven at 350 degrees until the yolks are set for 8 to 10 minutes. Remove from the oven and serve. *Serves 4*

Scanty South of the Border Chorizo & Cheese Pudding with White Corn Madeline's

Our Cinco de Mayo brunch was an anticipated yearly event. My favorite part was arranging a special, colorful centerpiece for the table. As I draped the bright, yellow cloth over the tabletop, I tied the red, lime-green, and magenta napkins together. I positioned my naked, tanned body down the center of the table, and then, removing the giant dahlia from the vase, I placed it in my hair. I then placed several flowers between my toes and fingers. Scantily covering myself with the napkins, I called to him to bring his chorizo and come to breakfast.

Chorizo & Cheese Pudding
- 8 corn tortillas cut into 8 wedges
- 1 tablespoon butter
- 2 cups green onions, sliced thin
- 2 lbs fresh, bulk Chorizo
- 2 ½ cups milk
- 1½ teaspoons dried mustard
- ¼ cup diced cilantro
- 1 lb Monterey Jack cheese grated
- 5 eggs
- 1 teaspoon nutmeg
- 3 diced tomatoes
- 2 diced green chilies

Place the chorizo in a pan and cook until browned, breaking it up into chunks as it cooks. Remove the chorizo from the pan and set it aside to cool. Butter a 9x13 casserole with a tablespoon of butter. Beginning with the tortilla wedges, layer the wedges, green onion, green chilies, tomatoes, and sausage, sprinkling the cheese between each layer. Beat the eggs with milk, dry mustard, nutmeg, and cilantro. Pour over the top and cover. Refrigerate overnight. Bake in a 350-degree oven for one hour. *Serves 8*

White Corn Madeline's
- 2 tablespoons minced white onion
- ¼ teaspoon cayenne pepper
- 3 tablespoons butter
- 3 tablespoons sugar
- ¾ cup white corn meal
- 1 1/2 teaspoons baking powder
- ¼ cup flour
- 1 egg
- ½ teaspoon salt
- 1 cup half & half
- 1 ear white corn kernels removed
- 1 tablespoon oil

Melt the butter in a pan over medium heat. Add the onions and sauté. Remove from the heat and set aside to cool. Combine the corn meal, flour, salt, corn kernels, cayenne, sugar, and baking powder in a bowl. Stir in the onion, egg, and half & half.

Grease each Madeline mold with oil. Spoon the batter into each mold. Bake in a preheated oven at 400 degrees for fifteen minutes. *Makes 8 Madeline's*

Juicy Peppered Bacon Twists and Chive Eggs

Knowing he would be arriving soon, I wanted to create a "Knock- Your- Socks- Off Breakfast." I fantasized about seductively removing his socks and kissing my way up his firm, muscular legs until I reached his head. This stimulating vision was most enjoyable as the thoughts of nibbling on the hot twisted meat brought me an anxious sensation.

Peppered Bacon Twists
- 8 slices partially cooked peppered bacon
- 1 fresh pineapple
- 16 toothpicks

Peel and core the fresh pineapple. Cut the pineapple in half lengthwise and then cut each half into four wedges. Wrap a strip of bacon around each wedge and secure with toothpicks. Broil the bacon and pineapple, turning it as it browns. Remove from the broiler and keep warm. *Serves 6 to 8*

Chive Eggs
- 1 dozen eggs
- 1½ cup cream
- 4 oz Garlic Feta cheese
- 2 tablespoons butter
- 1 bunch chives
- ½ teaspoon paprika
- salt and pepper to taste

Butter a 9 x 13 baking pan. Beat the eggs until thoroughly combined and pour into the baking pan. Season the eggs with salt and pepper. Pour the cream over the top. Crumble the Feta cheese and sprinkle over the eggs. Dice the bunch of chives and sprinkle over the cheese. Season this mixture with paprika. Bake in a 350-degree oven for approximately 20 minutes. *Serves 6 to 8*

Passionate Prawns Hollandaise

Slipping into my burgundy satin robe, I told him that I would be right back. Upon my return, I saw him sitting on the edge of the bed with the lemon-colored sheets draped loosely over his loins. A lock of his brunette hair was resting on his high forehead. Removing the belt from my robe, I knelt on the bed behind him and covered his eyes. After securing it, I positioned myself on his lap. Taking a morsel of food from the tray, I placed it in his mouth. I then asked him to identify it. It was a ceremony we went through any time I was introducing a new dish. Since his answer was incorrect, I smeared the sauce over my lips and passionately kissed him. Gently opening his mouth, I placed another tidbit of food on his tongue and instructed him to chew. His answer was correct, so the blindfold came off, as did the robe and sheet. Breakfast was served!

- ½ cube butter
- 2 toes minced garlic
- 1 lb 16-20 prawns washed, de-veined, and patted dry
- 2 large croissants halved and toasted
- lemon butter (2 tablespoons butter mixed with 2 teaspoons of lemon zest)
- 12 hot steamed asparagus spears
- 4 hot poached eggs
- 1 tablespoon chopped dill

Melt the butter in a pan until it foams. Add the chopped garlic and stir. Quickly sauté the prawns in the sizzling butter one layer at a time until they turn pink. Remove from the pan and place on a dish. Lay each croissant half on a plate. Butter each half with lemon butter and lay 3 spears of asparagus on top of the croissant.

Top with a poached egg and place 4 prawns on top of the egg. Cover with the sauce and sprinkle the fresh dill on top. *Serves 4*

Hollandaise Sauce
- ½ cup butter
- ¼ cup tablespoons lemon juice
- 1 tablespoon capers
- 3 beaten egg yolks
- salt to taste and a pinch of cayenne
- 1 tablespoon white wine

Melt the butter in a small saucepan at a very low temperature and keep warm. Heat the lemon juice in a small pan and keep warm also. Using a double boiler, place 3 beaten egg yolks over hot water and whisk until they begin to thicken. Add the tablespoon of wine and whisk again. Beat in the warmed lemon juice. Remove the double boiler from the heat and beat the sauce well with the wire whisk. Continue to beat constantly while slowly adding the melted butter. Add the salt and cayenne and beat until the sauce is thick. Fold in the capers. Serve at once. *Makes 1 cup*

CHAPTER NINE
WET AND WILD
Beverages

In my dream, the air is heavy with the fragrance of ripe grapes. Engulfed by moonlight, I meet him in the vineyard to dance among the vines as we pick the fruit for our first wine.

Fanciful Cranberry Margaritas

Margaritas are our favorite beverage. Experimenting with the flavors and scents of fruity additions became a game for us. Whoever designed the best margarita could choose the sexual activity for that day. This prize concoction made me the all-time champion.

- 1 bag cranberries
- 2 cups sugar
- 2 tablespoons lime juice

Place the cranberries, sugar, and lime juice in the bowl of a processor. Pulse until finely chopped 5-6 times. Remove the cranberries from the processor bowl and place them into another bowl. Cover and refrigerate. *Makes 2 cups*

Per Margarita
- 1 jigger Tequila
- ½ jigger Triple Sec
- ½ jigger lime juice

Place liquid ingredients in a blender. Add 1 tablespoon of cranberry mixture for each Margarita. Add six to eight ice cubes and process to a slushy consistency. Pour into a frosted glass that has had the rim coated with lime juice and dipped in salt.

Sensational Grape Juice

The beautiful deep purple color of the grapes dangling from the arbor over the back patio was beckoning for us to pick them. As I put my arms above my head and snipped the fruit, his hands slid up and down my sides in a playful fashion. Turning to face him, I peeled a grape and popped it in his mouth. As I rubbed another across his lips, it burst, and the juice covered his lips and chin. Pressing my lips on his, I tasted the sweet, subtle nectar. Then, as if we were reading each other's minds, we began to take turns gently smashing clumps of grapes against one another's bare skin. This sensuous tasting spurred us on to use the entire basket of grapes. Grape juice has never tasted so good.

- 5 lbs dark-skinned grapes with seeds, de-stemmed.
- sugar to taste

Wash the grapes. Place them in a non-aluminum pan. Cover with boiling water. Heat over a low flame and simmer until the fruit is very soft, stirring occasionally. As the fruit simmers, cut through the grapes with a knife to release some of the juice. When the fruit is soft, remove it from the heat and strain it between two layers of cheesecloth. Discard the pulp. Chill the juice for 1 to 2 days in the refrigerator, and then strain it once more. Taste the juice for sweetness. If a sweeter taste is desired, heat to a simmer and add sugar to taste.

If desired, juice may be frozen into ice cube trays and stored in zip-lock bags. *Makes ½ gallon*

Thought-provoking Apricot Champagne

As I leaned against the trunk of the apricot tree, he sliced open a piece of its' firm fruit. Asking me to close my eyes, he then covered my lids with each half of the pitted fruit. Pulling my tank top up, he unfastened my lacy bra, and I felt the warm fruit against my bare chest. As he pressed against me, I felt his thumb lower my bottom lip, which caused my mouth to open gently. He slowly poured champagne into my mouth, stopping for a wet kiss after every swallow. Taking the halves from my skin, he gingerly poured some champagne into each hollowed section. He sipped the beverage with much pleasure from this vessel. Knowing that apricots are my favorite fruit, he introduced me to a new method of enjoying them.

- 4 dried apricots
- 1 bottle champagne
- 4 tablespoons Grand Marnier

Place 4 dried apricots into a small pot. Barely covered with champagne. Cook over low heat until the champagne is absorbed and the apricots are plump and soft. Remove from the heat and place in a bowl. Refrigerate the apricots and champagne until chilled. Place each apricot into a champagne glass. Fill with champagne about ¾ of the way. Float a tablespoon of Grand Mariner in the champagne. *Serves 4*

Fuzzy Sprints

Anointing my body with the scent of peach lotion and peach body powder was a favorite pass time for him. Once the powder was applied, he would draw designs on my skin. Rubbing his hands over my fuzzy peach and tilting my head back, he would feed me delectable slices of this unpeeled fruit. Combined with a tasty wine, this made an unimaginable aphrodisiac.

- 1 cup water and dry white wine
- ½ cup vanilla sugar
- 1 basket raspberries
- 2 tablespoons Grand Mariner
- 2 white peaches, reserve 4 slices
- 1 bunch mint
- 16 oz club soda or white wine

Syrup

Mix 1 cup of water and dry white wine with the vanilla sugar and place over low heat, cooking until the liquid is reduced to ¾ cup. Remove the pan from the heat, place the liquid in a container, and chill. Coarsely mash the raspberries and mix with the chilled syrup and the Grand Mariner. Slice the white peaches and place an equal amount into the bottoms of 4 wine glasses. Place 2 tablespoons of syrup in the bottom of the glass and fill with crushed ice. Add club soda or white wine. Lay a peach slice and a sprig of mint on top of the ice. *Serves 4*

Fizzing Virgin

Cherry picking was a fun but exhausting adventure. Sitting in the hot tub and letting the bubbles caress our fatigued bodies was not the only treat of the evening. Sipping a refreshing and soothing concoction highlighted our adventure. He has a special way of tying the cherry stem into a knot using only his tongue

while it is in my mouth. This was yet another trick he could do using only his tongue.

- 16 ounces club soda
- 1-quart cherry juice
- 8 fresh cherries
- 8 strips lemon peel

Fill a tall glass with ice. Fill the glass ¾ of the way with cherry juice. Add the club soda until it reaches the top of the glass. Float a lemon peel and fresh cherry on top. *Serves 8*

Invigorating Jamaican Rum Punch

Vacationing in Jamaica was delicious! We lived on fresh tropical fruit and our "special love potion of the day." After drinking a few of these beverages from hollow coconuts, our inhibitions melted. My sarong became our blanket. His coconut became a vessel to bath ourselves from as we washed the sticky nectar from each other's bodies. Love potions aren't just for drinking!

- 1-quart dark rum
- 1 quart of lemon and orange juices
- 1 cup apricot brandy
- ¼ cup grenadine
- 1 cup tea syrup

To make the tea syrup, mix 1 cup of very strong brewed tea and 1 cup of sugar. Cook over medium heat until the liquid turns to a syrup consistency. Cool before adding to the remaining ingredients. Combine all the remaining ingredients and let set for 3 days. *Serves 14*

Comforting Ginger Beer

The aroma of whole cloves and lime peel simmering on the antique stove keyed up our senses. Wrapped only in a down comforter, we huddled together in front of the crackling fire anticipating what was to come. Within minutes our body heat was so intense that the rumpled comforter lay in a heap on the floor. After our frolic on the floor, we sipped this invigorating mixture. Once again, our excitement was stirred. What an enjoyable way to celebrate autumn!

- ¼ lb. ginger washed and sliced thin
- juice and rind of 1 lime
- 6 whole cloves
- 10 cups water
- 4 cups white sugar
- 2 tablespoons diced crystallized ginger

Put the ginger slices, lime peel, lime juice, cloves, and sugar in cold water in a pot. Bring to a boil and boil for 5 minutes. Remove from the heat and let it stand overnight covered. Strain the mixture. Chill and serve over ice. *Serves 6*

CHAPTER TEN
FIRE OF DESIRE
Condiments

Lying atop the grand stump in the Sequoia grove, with the moonbeams casting shadows across his cheeks, I softly kiss the beads of sweat, which gently roll from his chest. The heat of the bonfire is less equal to the fiery passion felt as we lose ourselves in the fire of desire, sweltering, spicy, hot, and sticky. Not only are these condiments desirable, but they also enhance the finishing touches to any meal

Chardonnay Butter & Merlot Butter

In the winter, on Friday nights, we always enjoyed dining in front of the fireplace. We considered this a weekly date. He would have beef, and I would have fish. Smearing this butter over our "top and tail" was always a mouth-watering eroticism escapade.

Chardonnay Butter
- 1 cube soft butter
- 1 teaspoon lemon thyme leaves and lemon zest
- 1 toe diced garlic
- 1 tablespoon chardonnay
- ¼ teaspoon white pepper

Mix all ingredients in a bowl. Place into a butter mold or shape into a 4-inch log and wrap in plastic wrap. Place into the

refrigerator until hardened. Remove from the mold or cut into ½-inch slices and place on top of chicken or fish. Serves 8

Merlot Butter
- 1 cube soft butter
- 1 teaspoon diced flat leaf parsley
- 1 diced garlic toe
- 1 tablespoon coarse, ground black pepper
- 1 tablespoon Merlot

Mix all ingredients in a bowl. Place into a butter mold or shape into a 4-inch log and wrap in plastic wrap. Place into the refrigerator until hardened. Remove from the mold or cut into ½-inch slices and place on top of the beef. Serves 8

Spicy Ketchup

That guy of mine loves to put ketchup on everything! He did admit that I was the spiciest dish he had ever tasted!

- 2 overripe diced tomatoes
- 1 roasted red bell pepper
- 2 tablespoons tomato paste
- 1 medium diced red onion
- 2 bay leaves
- 1 tablespoon fennel seed
- 4 tablespoons minced garlic
- ½ teaspoon dried red pepper
- ½ cup brown sugar
- ½ cup red wine
- 2 tablespoons apple cider vinegar
- ½ teaspoon ground cumin, coriander, and cilantro

Place the tomatoes with the juice and all other ingredients in a pot. Bring this to a boil, reduce the heat, and simmer into it is reduced by one-third, approximately 30 minutes. Remove from the heat and allow the mixture to cool. Remove the bay leaf and place the ingredients in a food processor. Puree and season with salt to taste. Chill. *Makes 3 cups*

Mint Pesto

Another absolute turn-on is when he kisses me after nibbling on mint leaves. The mouth-watering taste of the mint oil, coupled with the gentle prodding stimulation from my olfactory sense, leaves my mouth open and yearning for more of his tasty kisses.

- 2 cups lightly packed mint leaves
- 2 tablespoons raspberry vinegar
- 1 tablespoon pine nuts
- 2 cloves garlic
- ¼ cup extra virgin olive oil
- salt and pepper to taste

Place the mint leaves, pine nuts, and garlic in a processor. Process the mixture until ground. Add the oil in a slow study stream. Season the ingredients with salt and pepper. This is a nice accompaniment to lamb and poultry. *Makes 2 cups*

Hot-Tee Horseradish

My mouth is always ready for a hot sensation. He can heighten my experience by adding a little more of the root!

- 1 cup heavy cream
- 2 - 4 tablespoons fresh-grated horseradish

Place beater and bowl in the freezer. When they are well chilled, remove them from the freezer and place the cold cream in the bowl. Whip until stiff. Fold in the horseradish. This is great on prime rib and other beef dishes. *Makes 2 cups*

Cranberry Jalapeno Chutney (For pork, duck, and turkey)

He is a thigh man! My honey especially loves this fiery sweet combination rubbed all over my inner, hot, throbbing thighs. This

heated creation leaves his forehead sweating and his heart pumping!

- ½ cup of fresh cilantro
- 1 package fresh cranberries
- 1 lime
- 2 tablespoons honey
- 1 minced and seeded Jalapeno pepper

Place the cranberries in a processor and process until coarsely chopped. Remove from the processor bowl and place into a medium size bowl, and set aside. Cut the ends off the lime. Wash the outside of the lime and dry. Cut into eights and place in the processor bowl, and process until finely diced. Add to the cranberries along with the honey and jalapeno. Mix. Place the cilantro leaves in the processor and pulse 3 or 4 times. Add to the cranberry mixture. Combine well. Refrigerate for several hours or overnight. Serve with poultry or pork at room temperature or chilled. *Makes 2 cups*

Orange Rosemary Béarnaise Sauce (For lamb, fish, and chicken)

What a combination! The potent smell of the orange entices him to savor every drop as he licks it from the nap of my neck. Tickling his nude body with sprigs of fresh rosemary whet his appetite. I normally end up making a double batch. One for our dinner and one for us!

- 2 tablespoons finely chopped white onion
- 2 tablespoons chardonnay vinegar
- ¼ cup finely chopped mint leaves
- 1 large egg
- ½ cup butter
- 1 tablespoon fresh orange juice

Place the onion, vinegar, and mint in a pot and cook over medium heat, uncovered, until most of the liquid has evaporated. Reduce heat to simmer. Add the butter one tablespoon at a time and continue cooking until the butter is melted. Combine the egg and the juice in a food processor. With the motor running, add the butter mixture in a slow, steady stream. Serve warm or at room temperature. This is great with salmon or lamb. *Makes ½ cup*

Lemon Curd Sauce (For the fruit of the season and breakfast bread)

This lightly sweetened sauce is excellent over fruit and muffins. Smearing a little of this over his biceps left me feeling a little wet and sticky as I playfully licked it off.

- 6 beaten egg yolks
- juice of 4 lemons
- 1 cup sugar
- zest 1 lemon
- 1 cup cream whipped
- 1 cup vanilla sugar
- 1 stick butter

Place the egg yolks in a pot and add the lemon juice and sugar. Combine well. Cook over low heat or a double boiler, constantly stirring until thick, about 10 minutes. Remove from the heat and place the curd in a bowl. Cover with a piece of plastic wrap and let it set until the mixture slightly cools. Remove the plastic wrap and stir the butter, one tablespoon at a time, into the mixture until it is fully incorporated. Add the zest. Re-cover with plastic wrap and chill. Mix equal parts of fresh whipping cream with the curd. Serve. *Makes 2 cups of curd*

Maytag Blue Sauce (For grilled Portabella mushrooms and baked potatoes)

After drawing me a hot bubble bath, he brings me a frosty glass of chilled French wine. Before he softly scrubs my back, I taste the blue cheese spread from his fingertips. Another sip of wine, and he is in the tub with me. The aroma of steaks being grilled in the fireplace penetrates my nostrils. Is it the wine, or do I feel another arousing penetration?

- 2 cups thinly sliced red onion
- boiling water
- ½ cup olive oil
- ½ lemon juiced
- ½ teaspoon salt
- 1 teaspoon garlic powder
- ¼ teaspoon powdered mustard, paprika, and white pepper
- 1 cup Maytag Blue Cheese, crumbled

Place the onions in a shallow bowl. Cover with boiling water. When the onions are wilted, pour off the water. Shake the onions to remove any excess water. Mix the remaining ingredients until thoroughly combined. Put the onions back in a bowl and place the dressing on top. Let it set for 2 hours. *Makes 1 cup*

CHAPTER ELEVEN
MOONLIGHT MORSELS FOR TWO
Midnight Snacks

The ultimate climax----when all was said and done and the celestial lunar orb was rotating across the night sky, we found our bodies satiated, our spirits elevated, our minds blissful, and our emotions peaceful. Oh, what a sublime feeling! Our last indulgence of the day was highlighted by the mouth-watering portions that only two people can share!

Waxing Moon Roasted Pepper & Artichoke Heart Dip

The moonlight shimmering on the surface of the lake was visible enough to catch sight of our silhouettes. Skinny dipping after midnight was filled with laughter and surprise. Each time the experience was unique yet special. One thing that remained the same was the pounding of my heart each time he pressed his nude wet body against mine as we floated across the lagoon. Roasting the peppers on the beach as we cuddled in our soft beach towels was the finishing touch to an enchanting dip.

- ¼ cup mayonnaise and sour cream
- 2 tablespoons roasted chopped red bell pepper
- 2 marinated artichoke hearts diced
- ¼ cup grated parmesan cheese
- 12 tortilla chips

Mix the above ingredients, except the chips, together in a microwave bowl. Cook the dip on high flame for one minute or until thoroughly heated. This dip may also be served at room temperature. Serve with tortilla chips. *Makes one cup.*

Waning Moon Crab Spread with Endive

With the classical music low in the background, we were in deep concentration as he pondered how to jump me. Being the woman that I am, I was determined not to let him get over me. Although I did not want a crab on my hands, I knew he had to make the right moves. But alas, checkmate. I won!!

- 3 oz. cream cheese softened
- 2 ounces crab meat
- Teaspoon white Worcestershire sauce and fresh lemon juice
- ½ teaspoon lemon pepper and salt
- 1/3-pound Belgian endive leaves
- Teaspoon chopped dill

Mix the cream cheese, Worcestershire Sauce, and lemon juice in a bowl. Fold in the crab meat and season with salt and lemon pepper. Mound ½ teaspoon on the stem end of each endive leaf. Garnish with the dill. *Makes 8 pieces*

Blue Moon Blueberry Sundae

After playing the once famous hit, "Blue Moon," for the seventh time, I finally admitted that I was blue for my baby. After a seductive phone call, he welcomed my invitation for a midnight nibble. Lapping up the ice cream always left my tongue frigid

and without sensation. The warmth of the berries brought it back to life. This time I promised not to bite before I licked.

- 2 cups blueberries set 4 aside
- 4 scoops vanilla ice cream
- cup sugar
- 2 mint leaves

Blend the berries and sugar until smooth. Place in a pan and bring the berry mixture to a boil. Cook for 5 minutes. Remove from the stove and place in a bowl. Allow cooling until slightly warm, about 15 minutes.

In the meantime, place two scoops into a frosted wide-mouth champagne glass. Repeat with the remaining ice cream. Place in the freezer. When the sauce is cool, pour it over the ice cream. Garnish with the remaining berries and mint leaves. *Serves 2*

Full Moon Baked Brie with Asian Pears in a Cinnamon Sugar Pastry

Sleeping under the stars on a full moon night is a magnificent occurrence. Counting the endless stream of shooting stars while wrapped up with him in his sleeping bag seemed heavenly. After a while, I wasn't sure what I was seeing and what I was feeling. Wrapping his pear in my pastry is a most delicious reward!

- 1 pound wheel of Brie
- ½ Asian pear sliced thin
- sheet puff pastry thawed
- 1 teaspoon cinnamon and sugar mixed together
- ½ baguette sliced into ¼ inch pieces

Lay the Brie on a parchment-lined cookie sheet and unwrap. Place the apples on top of the Brie. Cut the puff pastry in half. Sprinkle half of the sugar mixture over the Asian pear. Place the puff pastry on top and fold it to enclose the cheese. Moisten the edges with water and place under the wheel of Brie. Sprinkle the remaining sugar mixture on the puff pastry. Bake in a preheated 400 oven for 15-10 minutes. Serve with sliced baguettes. *Makes one wheel*

Man in the Moon Three Cheese & Grape Spread

On nights like this, when the moonlight lit the entire sky, we loved to drive our vintage convertible to the top of the ridge to gaze at the moon. We sat in the back, his arms tightly around me, and we held each another. Not a word was spoken. The sounds of our heavy breathing and low guttural moans echoed

across the canyon. I prepared this savory snack the first night we initiated this spot!

- 2 oz. Roquefort cheese, cream cheese, and white Cheddar cheese
- 6 red grapes cut into quarters
- ½ cup finely chopped walnuts
- 6-8 crackers

Blend the cheeses until well combined. Fold in the grapes. Line a ramekin dish with plastic wrap so that it hangs about 2 inches over the sides. Place the cheese in the dish and refrigerate for 10 minutes. Remove from the refrigerator and lift the cheese out of the dish by pulling up the plastic. Scatter the walnuts on a plate. Place the cheese on the walnuts and roll around. When the cheese is well coated, place the ball on a plate and surround it with crackers. *Makes ½ cup*

Harvest Moon Fruit Sticks with White Chocolate Glaze

One hot sultry night in September with no breeze in the air, we found ourselves lying on top of the hay stack inside the orchard. The enormous moon, with its bright yellow color, beckoned for us to reach out and touch it. This night was set for romance! One kiss led to another, and before we knew it, we were wrestling in the hay generating our own heat. Later, as he pulled the straw from my hair, I presented this fruit to him once again.

- 6 apricots pitted
- ¼ pineapple cored and peeled and cut into 12 chunks
- 12 cherries
- 3 kiwis peeled and cut into 12 slices
- 6 skewers (cut thin branches from fruit trees and leave a couple of leaves at the end of each branch)
- 4 oz. white chocolate grated
- 1 tablespoon cream
- 2 tablespoons mint julienne

Place the chocolate and cream in a bowl and microwave at full power until melted, about 45 seconds. Remove from the microwave and stir. Set aside.

Skewer the fruit alternating the types and allowing two pieces of each fruit per skewer. Brush with the chocolate and place on a serving dish. Garnish with mint. *Makes 12 skewers*

Paper Moon Prosciutto & Port Peach Chunks

Pouring the last of the Port from the bottle, he placed the dripping candle in the neck and invited me outside. As we sat on the terrace, our eyes were fixated upon the colossal moon. The wax from the candle began to drip brilliant colors over the jug. The flame was motionless. As he began to kiss my throat, my eyes closed and hearing myself murmur a soft sultry moan, I could see

a lump pressing against my lips. The meat was soft and pliable, peachy in color, and ever so juicy.

- 3 thin slices Proscuitto
- 1 peach seeded and cut into 6 thick slices
- ¼ cup port
- mint leaves

Lay the peach slices in a bowl. Pour the Port on the peaches and let set for 10 minutes. Turn the peaches over after 5 minutes.

Cut the Proscuitto in half. Wrap a slice of Proscuitto around each peach slice. Place on a dish and pour the Port into a small bowl. Place the Port in the middle of the peach slices. Garnish with mint leaves. *Makes 6 pieces*

Half Moon Curried Nuts

After midnight and still unable to sleep, we decided to watch old movies. As he slipped the disc into the DVD player, I decided to concoct this sizzling nut fusion. Warm nuts seem to have a tendency to leave me sweltering!

- ¼ cup walnut oil
- 1 tablespoon curry powder and Worcestershire sauce
- 1 teaspoon salt and garlic powder
- dash cayenne
- 2 cups walnuts

Place all the ingredients, except the nuts, in a pan and cook over medium heat until hot. Add the walnuts and stir to coat. Pour the nuts onto a cookie sheet lined with parchment paper and bake in a 300-degree preheated oven for 10 minutes until crisp. Remove and allow the nuts to cool. *Makes 2 cups*

CHAPTER TWELVE
BITTERSWEET GOOD-BYES
Dessert

The ocean sunsets, dancing pink, purple, and gold across the incoming tide, and the low-flying seagulls escape the crashing surf. He tenderly licks the chocolate from my fingertips as I feel his warm lips embrace my bare shoulder.

Lusty Cream-Filled Cannoli

It was hard to say if most of the Chianti went into the cannoli dough or our wine glasses. Molding the dough around the cool, firm cylinder caused lustful thoughts to race through my mind. I wondered if he would accept my idea of a more pliable mold.

Cannoli Dough:
- ¼ cup sugar
- 2 cups flour
- 5 tablespoons butter
- 1 tablespoon Chianti
- ½ teaspoon salt
- 2 cups oil for frying

Mix the sugar and the butter in a large bowl. Add the salt and mix again. Add the flour, a cup at a time, and the Chianti, combining thoroughly. Place the dough in the refrigerator and chill for at least 2 hours.

Remove the dough from the refrigerator and roll it into a 9x12 rectangle. Cut into three-inch squares. Place the dough on the cannoli form folding it corner to corner. Seal with Chianti. Deep fry the form in the oil until golden brown. Remove from the oil and drain on paper towels. Set aside.

Ricotta Cream Filling
- 1 lb Ricotta cheese
- ¼ cup powdered sugar
- 1 teaspoon vanilla
- ½ teaspoon cinnamon oil
- 1 tablespoon cream

Place all the ingredients in a processor bowl EXCEPT cinnamon oil and process until thoroughly combined. Remove the mixture from the processor bowl and place it into a medium size bowl. Add the cinnamon oil a drop at a time, mixing well after each addition. Place mixture into a pastry bag and fill each cannoli shell. *Makes 10*

Creative Chocolate Clay Ravioli with Papaya Filling

After a few glasses of Chianti, the idea of creating a dessert together seemed exciting and fun. Once the clay was made, he began to form the soft, pliable dough around me. His artistic hands shaped the cups just as an experienced potter designs his ware.

Chocolate Clay
- 8 oz. semi-sweet chocolate coarsely chopped
- 3 tablespoons powdered sugar
- 1/3 cup light corn syrup

Heat the chocolate over a low flame in a copper pot or the top of a double boiler until melted, gradually adding the corn syrup. Add the powdered sugar and fold in until smooth. Fold onto parchment paper and spread out to a 9 x 12 rectangle as thinly as possible and as quickly as possible. Place in a refrigerator and chill.

Filling:
- 1 papaya peeled, seeded, and chopped
- 1 tablespoon orange zest

Mix the papaya and zest and place them in the refrigerator to chill.

Assembling
- 1 star fruit
- 2 stems of fresh mint

About an hour before serving, remove the chocolate from the refrigerator and thaw at room temperature until pliable. Cut the rectangle into three, three-inch strips and run through settings five and four on a pasta machine, one time each. Or roll the dough out using a rolling pin until 1/8 of an inch thickness. Cut each strip into three-inch squares. Place one square on a cutting board and put a tablespoon of the filling into the center, spreading the mixture almost to the edge. Place another square on top and pinch the sides closed using the tines of a fork. Place on a plate and garnish with fresh mint leave and a slice of star fruit. *Serves 9*

Calvados Apple Crepes with Caramel Sauce

Early Sunday evening, as we sat on the deck listening to the church bells ring in the distance, I placed these sweet apple concoctions before him. Sensually glancing over the bowl of shiny apples, he beckoned me to polish his forbidden fruit.

Crepes
- 4 whole eggs beaten
- 1 cup flour
- 1 tablespoon sugar
- 1 cup half & half
- ¼ teaspoon salt
- ¼ cup vegetable oil
- small amount of oil for cooking crepes

Beat the eggs in a bowl. Then add the sugar and salt. Beat again. Gradually whisk in the flour. Slowly pour in the half & half and the oil whisking continually. Set batter aside for 30 minutes. If the batter is too thick, add a little more half & half. Dip the ends of a paper towel into the oil and generously grease the crepe pan.

Place the crepe pan over medium heat and add ¼ cup of the batter, swirling the pan to form a rounded crepe. Adjust the heat if necessary so as to not burn the crepe. Repeat until all the batter is gone. Layer the crepes between sheets of waxed paper. Set the cooked crepes aside until ready to use.

Calvados Apples:
- 1 tablespoon butter
- 1 teaspoon ground cinnamon and cardamom
- 2 lbs tart apples peeled, cored, and thinly sliced
- 1/3 cup sugar
- ¼ cup Calvados

Melt the butter in a pan over medium heat. Add the apples and spices. Mix well and cook, occasionally stirring, until the apples are tender, about 5 minutes. Mix in the sugar and cook for 3 more minutes until the apple juice becomes thick and syrupy. Pour the Calvados over the apples and stir again. Remove from the heat.

Caramel Sauce:
- ¾ cup sugar
- ½ cup apple juice
- ¼ cup butter
- 1 tablespoon Calvados

Melt the sugar in a cast iron pan until golden brown and syrupy, about 5 minutes. Note: (Once the sugar begins to melt, turn the heat to low and constantly stir for about 3 minutes. The longer you cook the sugar, the browner the syrup will become and the stronger the flavor will be. Watch the sugar very closely as it changes color quickly and it will taste scorched if it becomes too dark.) Remove the caramel from the heat and stir in the apple juice. Add the butter and Calvados and mix well. Place over low heat and stir about 5 more minutes or until it has re-melted.

Assemble
- 8 pecan halves

Place a warm crepe on a plate. Add two tablespoons of the apple mixture to the center of each crepe and spread it along the length of the crepe. Fold the crepe in half. Spoon the caramel sauce on top. Garnish with pecan halves. *Makes 8*

Intimate Chocolate Pate with Zinfandel Peppercorn Sauce

It was now my turn to wear the red silk blindfold. As he lightly brushed my cheekbones, eyelids, chin, and throat, the tingling sensation was only enhanced as he carefully dipped the ends of his paintbrush in the melted chocolate and continued this sexy scenario over the rest of my body. Using the tip of his index finger, I could feel him lightly drawing circles on the end of my nose with the pate. Sensuously outlining the contours of my lips with the chocolate sent chills up and down my spine. Then with heated passion, he pressed his lips forcefully over mine. Placing his strong masculine hands around my fragile wrists, he bent me back onto the bed and kissed me with meaning and passion! Removing the blindfold, I positioned my finger into our dessert and began to finger paint his body. I could feel the chocolate slide over our mouths as we continued to kiss. As he plunged his warm, moist tongue over mine, the rich, sweet taste of the chocolate was very prominent. Feeling my entire body shiver with anticipation of what was to come was thrilling.

Chocolate Pate:
- 3 ½ pounds of dark chocolate
- 15 egg yolks
- 10 oz. butter
- 1 ½ cups powdered sugar
- 3 ½ cups heavy cream
- *10 oz dark rum or Grand Mariner
- zest of a grapefruit

Place the chocolate, butter, and cream on the top of a double boiler and melt over simmering water. When melted, place in a large bowl and add the yolks one at a time beating well after each. Add the powdered sugar, liquor, and zest. Mix well. Line a loaf pan with waxed paper. Place the mixture in the pan and let set in the refrigerator for 24 hours. When ready to serve, lift the wax paper from the pan and place it on a cutting board. Using a fishing line or piano wire, slice the pate into ½ slices. *Serves 16* *orange juice may be substituted for liquor.

Zinfandel Sauce:
- 1 tablespoon black peppercorns
- 1 bottle of Zinfandel
- 1 cup sugar

Combine the peppercorns, wine, and sugar in a saucepan. Cook over medium heat until two cups remain for about 30 minutes. Stir often with a wooden spoon to prevent scorching. Remove from the heat and place into a bowl. When cool, refrigerate for at least two hours. *Makes 2/3 cup*

Assembling:
- 1 basket raspberries
- 1 bunch mint

Place a tablespoon of the wine sauce on a dessert plate and swirl. Add a slab of the pate. Garnish with fresh raspberries and a mint leaf.

Zorro's Blanco Chocolate Cheesecake

Spreading the shaving cream from my inner thigh to my ankle heightened my sense of arousal as his hands slid up and down my legs. Each time he made a fresh path with the razor, I would reward him with a nibble of cheesecake. The best part, of course, was when he wiped my legs clean with a hot, steamy towel. The sensation of this combination always led to a new experience!

Cheesecake
- 1-pound white chocolate finely chopped
- 1½ pounds cream cheese
- 1 cup sugar
- 4 beaten eggs
- 1 ½ cups sour cream
- 1 tablespoon fresh lemon juice
- 1 tablespoon Torani Orgeat (almond syrup)

Melt the chocolate in the top of a double boiler until smooth. Remove the pan from the heat and place the chocolate in a bowl. Set aside to cool. In the bowl of a processor, mix the sugar and eggs until well combined. Add the cream cheese and sour cream and beat again, mixing well. Stir in the almond syrup and lemon juice. Add the chocolate and combine well.

Grease a nine-inch spring form pan. Place a sheet of greased parchment paper inside the pan and press it into the sides and the bottom of the pan to make a tight fit. Trim away any excess paper that remains, allowing a 2-inch overhang around the rim of the pan. Pour the batter into the pan. Place a pan larger than the spring form pan on the bottom rack of the oven and fill with 3 inches of boiling water. Place the cheesecake on the middle rack and bake in a preheated oven at 400 degrees baking for 10 minutes. Then reduce the heat to 300 degrees and cook for another 40 minutes. Remove from the oven and cool for 10 minutes. Spread the topping over the cheesecake and bake at 350 degrees for 5 more minutes.

Topping
- 2 cups sour cream
- 2 tablespoons vanilla sugar
- 1 tablespoon Torani Orgeat

Mix these ingredients in a bowl and spread over the surface of the cheesecake

Remove the cheesecake from the oven and cool on a wire rack. Place it in the refrigerator and chill overnight. Remove the cheesecake and open the springs on the side of the pan. Lift the bottom of the cheesecake away from the sides and place it on a serving tray. Trim the parchment paper flush with the sides of the cheesecake. Cut into wedges and serve. *Makes 12 slices*

Sexy Shortbread Squares with Peaches in a Champagne Sabayon Sauce

Sitting on the grassy knoll and watching the rushing water spill over the rocks was such a relaxing occasion. Lying back onto the prickly blades of grass, I closed my eyes and listened to the falling water. Feeling a tug on the zipper of my pants, I looked up to see the clasp between his teeth as he pulled my zipper down. I could feel his hot breath through the sheer fabric of my panties. He laid a few slices of peach on my stomach, which he gently devoured. Working his way up to my mouth, he kissed me fiercely. I could taste the champagne on the insides of his mouth. It was sweet from the flavor of peaches. Sitting up to take a drink of champagne, we clicked our glasses and made a peachy toast to our sexual future.

Shortbread:
- ½ lb powdered sugar
- 1 lb butter
- 1½ lbs. cake flour

Place the butter and powdered sugar in the bowl of a processor and mix until thoroughly combined. Add the cake flour and continue to process until a ball forms around the inside of the bowl. Remove the ball from the bowl. Roll the dough between two sheets of wax paper until a 9 x 13-inch rectangle has been formed. Place on a cookie sheet or in a 9 x 13 pan and bake in a preheated oven at 375 degrees for 12 to 15 minutes. Remove the shortbread from the oven and set it aside to cool. When cool, cut into three-inch squares.

Champagne Sabayon Sauce:
- 4 egg yolks
- ½ cup powdered sugar
- ¾ cup champagne
- zest of 1 lime

In the top of a double boiler, combine the yolks, sugar, champagne, and zest. Beat this mixture over the heat until it triples in volume, about 5 minutes. Serve warm.

- 3 whole peaches peeled and sliced
- 1 cup champagne

Place the peaches and champagne in a pan and poach over medium heat until the peaches are soft. Remove peaches from the liquid with a slotted spoon and place them in a bowl. Set aside.

Assemble
- zest of two limes

Place a shortbread square on a plate. Place a spoonful of the Champagne Sabayon Sauce on top. Place three slices of peaches in the center of the sauce. Garnish with the strands of lime zest.
Serves 6

Exciting Espresso –Panache Torte

I love picking him up from the airport after one of his business trips. Since he usually flies the "Red Eye," I knew my welcome home gift would be most appreciated. Pulling up to the curb, I handed him a steamy Latté as he entered the car. He discovered that I was only dressed in my soft velvet coat when he slid his hands inside to feel my coffee-colored skin.

Torte
- 8 oz semi-sweet chocolate pieces
- 1 cup of sugar
- ½ cup strong coffee
- 1 cup butter
- 4 beaten eggs
- ¼ lb espresso candy beans

In the top of a double boiler, melt the chocolate, sugar, and butter. Cool to room temperature. Add the coffee and mix well. Add the eggs and combine thoroughly. Fold in the coffee candy. Line an 8-inch spring form pan with buttered parchment paper. Pour in the batter and bake in a preheated oven at 350 degrees for 30 minutes. Remove from the oven and place on a rack to cool. Place the torte in the refrigerator overnight. Remove the sides of the spring form pan. Place a serving dish on top of the torte and flip it over. Remove the bottom of the spring form pan and parchment paper from the torte. Cut torte into wedges.

Optional: Can be served with shaved chocolate curls, slices of fresh fruit in season, or whipped cream. *Serves 8*

Fresh Strawberry Cream in White Chocolate Cups with Rose Petal Garni

As the steamy mist cleared from our steam bath, I saw our reflection in the mirror. His thick ebony hair and milky, white-chocolate skin pronounced his puffy pink-colored lips even more. My dark chocolate hair, milk chocolate skin, and red-colored lips complimented our merging contrast. Covering his fingers with whipped cream and placing them in my inviting mouth brought an arousing smile to his face. Cutting the strawberry halves, I colored his lips with the sweet red juice. With a gentle peck, the color was immediately transferred to my awaiting lips. I placed the berry in my mouth, rolled it around a few times, and passed it to his. The marriage of the cream and berry was a definite match, just as he and I were. The combination of the colors in this particular dessert reminds me of our match.

Chocolate Cups:
- ½ lb of white chocolate coarsely chopped
- 1/3 cup white corn syrup
- *3 tablespoons vanilla sugar

    Place chocolate on the top of a double boiler and melt over medium-low heat, gradually adding the corn syrup. Remove from the heat and add the vanilla sugar mixture until smooth. Pour chocolate into a parchment paper-lined 9x9 square pan and smooth with the back of a spoon. Place into the refrigerator and chill. About an hour before serving, remove it from the refrigerator and cut it into nine three-inch squares. Place each square inside a muffin tin and form it into a cup. Refrigerate until firm.

    * To make the vanilla sugar place one cup of sugar and a split vanilla bean into a jar. Store one week before using.

Strawberry Cream:
- 1 cup whipping cream
- ¼ cup vanilla sugar
- 2 baskets of strawberries washed, dried, and diced (set nine whole berries aside)

Whip the cream with the sugar until thick. Fold in the strawberries and set them aside.

Garni
- reserved strawberries
- 4 oz block of dark chocolate for grating

Assembling:
Remove each cup from the muffin tin and place it on a serving plate. Fill each cup half full with the strawberry cream. Wash nine strawberries and pat dry. Using the tip of a knife, cut each berry lengthwise into thin slices starting under the green leaves of the berry, not slice all of the ways through. Place each berry on top of the strawberry cream in a fan fashion. Decorate the top with long strips of grated chocolate. *Serves 9*

CHAPTER THIRTEEN
LET FOOD BE YOUR FOREPLAY, AND FOREPLAY BE YOUR FOOD

The search was on to find the treasure of aphrodisiac foods. These sexually powered Genitalia-shaped vegetables, herbs, and fruits would be sure to heighten our ardent sexual appetites.

Desirable Avocado Dressing

Untying the bows on my pink, sheer, lacy babydoll panties, he rolls me over on my tanned tummy. Like an artist with his canvas, he paints me with this creamy avocado dressing using his special tool. Savoring every luscious lick, he murmurs about how the halved avocado resembles the live canvas.

- 2 whole avocados peeled and seeded
- juice of a lemon
- ¼ cup lemon olive oil
- teaspoon salt
- 2 toes garlic
- cracked pepper

Place the garlic toes in a bowl and mash with the blunt end of a knife or a pestle. Sprinkle the salt on top and mix. Add the avocados and mash all the ingredients until they are well blended.

Stir in the lemon juice and olive oil. Combine thoroughly. Add the cracked pepper to taste and mix again. *Serves 4*

Voracious Vanilla Sugar

The lengthy willowy stick comes in all sizes, yet its shape remains the same. It can be used for many things, yet it has one special use. It imparts a unique taste to whoever is adventurous enough to taste it. As simple as this aphrodisiac is, by far, it is my favorite! I love it best when it is buried deep into the walls of sugary delights!!

- 5 lb. bag cane sugar
- 2 vanilla beans split down the middle
- peeling from orange without the white pith attached

Open the bag of sugar and place it in a glass jar. Bury the bean in the middle of the sugar. Cut the orange rind into 2-inch lengths and poke them into the sugar. Seal and let sit for a month. Use when a recipe calls for table sugar.

Bananas & Sherry Pound Cake Caressed with Caramel

After lighting the fireplace at the foot of the bathtub, I ease into the hot verbena-scented bubbles. Lying in his arms as the foam gently caresses our bodies, he lights the 69 fragrant rain candles that surround the tub. Teasing him with little morsels of this dessert only adds to our sensual soak. What could be better than a warm, firm banana swimming in a succulent sauce? Am I beginning to fall in love?

- 2 bananas cut into ½-inch chunks
- 2 slices of pound cake
- ½ cup hot caramel sauce divided

To assemble

Place one slice of pound cake on a plate. Lay the sliced bananas over the cake. Drizzle the hot sauce on the bananas. *Serves 2*

- Pound Cake
- cup butter
- 2 cups vanilla/orange sugar
- T vanilla
- 4 eggs separated
- 3 cups cake flour
- 2 teaspoons baking powder
- ¾ cup whole milk
- ¼ cup sherry

Beat the egg whites and set them aside. Cream the butter with the sugar. Add the vanilla and mix again. Add the yolks, one at a time, and beat until thoroughly combined. Add the baking powder and combine. Alternately add the flour and the milk and sherry, beating until smooth and creamy. Gently fold in the beaten egg whites. Place into a buttered loaf pan and bake at 350 for one hour. Cool completely. Remove from the pan and place on a plate. *Serves 10.*

Caramel Sauce
- cup sugar
- 2 ½ cups cream

Place the cream into a pan and simmer over medium-low heat. While this is simmering, add the sugar to a pan and cook over high heat, constantly stirring for about 5 minutes until it melts and turns a nice amber color. Slowly add the warm cream, reducing the heat to low, and continue to cook for about 2 minutes or until the caramel has melted.

Oysters Exhibitionist Style

We loved to greet the fishermen at the break of dawn as they navigated into the wharf with their daily catch. As they unloaded their baskets of magnificent mollusks onto the weathered dock, the fervent fish mongrels would scoop them up and cart them into the outdoor market, arranging them on mounds of shaved ice. It was always a surprise to discover what the daily wares would be. Today I had my own personal surprise for him! Slowly unzipping my coral trench coat, I pressed the curves of my naked body onto the glass partition that divided the seafood. I hungrily call for him. The thrill of anticipation came over me when I saw his clean-shaven face. Hurriedly he thrust the oysters into the mesh bag and placed a handful of the ice into my awaiting mouth. I let it gracefully spill from my parted ruby lips, the melting liquid descending over my chin and down onto my exposed chest. He thirstily drank these beads of water, and taking hold of my hot clammy hand, he beckoned for us to leave.

- 2 dozen oysters in the half shell
- ½ cup chili sauce
- ½ cup cocktail sauce
- juice of 1 lemon
- tablespoon grated horseradish
- dash tabasco
- 8 slices of bacon cut into thirds

Combine the sauces, lemon juice, horseradish, and Tabasco. Place the sauce over the oysters and place it on a parchment-lined baking sheet. Bake at 375 for 5 minutes. Remove from the oven and place a piece of bacon on top of each oyster. Return to the oven and bake until the bacon is brown. *Serves 4 as a main course or 8 as part of a buffet.*

Cucumber with Minted Yogurt Sauce

Grasping the sleek and sexy edible creation, he strokes it alongside my silky body. Casually flirting, he nudges the flimsy lingerie from my creamy shoulders with the tip of his go-tee-covered chin! Kissing them with his pronounced full lips melts me. His minted parted lips cool the hot sensation of his touch.

- Armenian cucumber cut into ¼ inch slices
- teaspoon salt
- 2 elephant garlic toes minced
- 2 cups plain yogurt
- ¼ cup dried mint
- fresh sprig mint

Place the garlic in a bowl. Add the salt and pound to make a paste. Add the yogurt and fold it into the garlic paste. Crumble the dried mint and add to the mixture. Stir to blend. Gently fold in the cucumbers. Garnish with a fresh mint sprig

Ginger Root Sauce

Digging up this aromatic root, I gingerly cut off the tender nubs that surround the thick core. Sauntering towards my outside kitchen, we meet on the threshold. He sweeps me up into his strong awaiting arms and carries me inside. He gently lays me on the cool onyx marble slab. I quickly pull him towards me. Placing the root in the palm of my throbbing hand, I soothingly wash it under the cool running water. The hot, tingling feeling overwhelms me as I place the entire interior into my mouth.

- 1 cup chicken broth
- 1 cup soy sauce
- 1 cup sake
- ¼ cup white sugar
- ¼ cup brown sugar
- 3 tablespoons minced ginger
- 1 tablespoon minced garlic
- ¼ teaspoon crushed red pepper (optional)
- 3 tablespoons corn starch

Dissolve the corn starch into the broth. Place into a saucepan and add the remaining ingredients. Place over a medium flame and cook until thick, stirring constantly. Remove and allow the sauce to cool. Baste meats and fish when grilling. *Makes 3 cups*

Intoxicating Fall Figs

After wine tasting on the autumn equinox, we popped open our favorite bottle of port and proceeded to build a fire in the outside hearth. Sipping the "nectar of the gods" as the dancing inferno mesmerized our gaze, he asked me to disrobe. Walking to the opposite side of the double-sided fireplace, he began to snap pictures through the red and yellow flames commanding me to lick my lips three times. Then he directed me to close my eyes. I could once again feel his presence near me. I felt the warm flesh enter my mouth and tasted the sweet fig batter as it hit the back of my throat.

- pound fresh figs coarsely chopped
- cup port wine
- zest of an orange
- 1 ½ cups vanilla sugar

- ½ cup pine nuts
- tablespoon anise seed
- 2 tablespoons sesame seeds

Place the wine, sugar, and zest into a pan. Cook over medium-low heat, occasionally stirring until the liquid becomes thick, approximately 10 minutes. Add the figs and cook until the figs are soft, about 5 minutes, stirring occasionally. Add the nuts and seeds and stir for about one minute. Remove from the heat. It can be served at room temperature or chilled. *Makes 2 ½ cups*

Although my young prince has given me passion and spirit, I sometimes wonder what life would be like with the mature, square-jawed, dimpled chin gentleman who smiles at me as we pass on the hiking trail by the edge of the lake. Has the King arrived? Has our May/December romance been interrupted?

CPSIA information can be obtained
at www.ICGtesting.com
Printed in the USA
BVHW011713081222
653774BV00034B/987